Polar Rearrangements

Laurence M. Harwood
The Dyson Perrins Laboratory and Merton College, University of Oxford

OXFORD   NEW YORK   TOKYO
OXFORD UNIVERSITY PRESS
1992

Oxford University Press, Walton Street, Oxford OX2 6DP

Oxford New York Toronto
Delhi Bombay Calcutta Madras Karachi
Petaling Jaya Singapore Hong Kong Tokyo
Nairobi Dar es Salaam Cape Town
Melbourne Auckland

and associated companies in
Berlin Ibadan

Oxford is a trademark of Oxford University Press

Published in the United Sates
by Oxford University Press, New York

A catalogue record for this book is available from the British Library

Library of Congress Cataloging in Publication Data

(Data available)

ISBN 0–19–855671–3
ISBN 0–19–855670–5 (Pbk)

Printed in Great Britain by
Information Press Ltd, Oxford, England

Series Editor's Foreword

Polar rearrangements have always fascinated organic chemists. They have provided rich and rewarding areas of study particularly in the fields of biosynthesis, mechanistic studies, and stereochemistry. Many reliable and useful synthetic methods have resulted from studies of polar rearrangements.

Oxford Chemistry Primers have been designed to provide concise introductions relevant to all students of chemistry and contain only the essential material that would normally be covered in an 8–10 lecture course. In this fifth primer of the series, Laurence Harwood has done a magnificent job in bringing together the wide range of mechanistic, stereochemical, and synthetic topics that make up polar rearrangements. This primer will be of interest to apprentice and master chemist alike.

Stephen G. Davies
The Dyson Perrins Laboratory, University of Oxford

Preface

In this short book I have attempted to bring together into the single category of 'polar rearrangements' those rearrangements which involve charge-separated intermediates or transition states. My aim has been to highlight basic principles and mechanistic similarities in order to facilitate comprehension of the various reaction types. Wherever possible, illustrative examples are taken from the areas of natural product chemistry or total synthesis to emphasize the relevance of the reactions for the organic chemist. Details of the discovery and mechanistic elucidation of the rearrangements have also been included to provide a historical background. The exercises at the end of each chapter have been designed to reinforce the various points discussed in the body of the text and I have included brief marginal notes to explain new technical terms as they appear. In this way I have tried to encapsulate the major features of all of the important polar rearrangements in one small book at a level which should make the contents accessible to students approaching this area for the first time. For those wishing to delve deeper than permitted by the confines of this work — and I hope that many will be stimulated to do just that — there are references to monographs and major reviews in the 'Further reading' sections which close each chapter.

I dedicate this book to Maureen, Mickle, and Spida, the three ladies in my life; the former for her inexhaustible love and support, the other two for purring all of the time, and all three for making life so delightful. I would also express my thanks to Sue Anslow who helped with proof-reading and to Steve Davies for convincing me to undertake what turned out to be a very enjoyable project.

Oxford   L. M. H.
August 1991

Contents

Oxford Chemistry Primers

1. Mechanism and theory

1.1 Introduction

What will this book cover?

Before launching into any discourse about polar rearrangements, it is first necessary to decide what kinds of reaction are to be included. This apparently simple objective immediately leads us into a multitude of pitfalls. It is impossible to compose a rigorous definition to encompass all reaction types which might conceivably fall within the framework of polar rearrangements without introducing a large degree of superfluity and far outgrowing the space available in this book. In any event rigorous definitions which become entangled in semantics are counter-productive to the aim of producing an accessible, easily read introduction to this fascinating area of chemistry.

Drawing the line between 'polar' and 'non-polar' rearrangements presents us with the need for making an arbitrary decision, because it can be justifiably argued that almost all organic reactions must display a certain amount of polarity. Therefore we will disregard simple polarisation effects and consider a polar rearrangement to be one in which some degree of formal charge separation occurs at the reacting sites prior to, or during, migration.

In its most general sense, a rearrangement may be defined as any chemical process involving the breaking and forming of σ- or π-bonds, in which an atom or group moves from one atom to another, resulting in structural reorganisation of the original molecule. We often talk about 'migrations' for such processes, but this terminology implies an intramolecular process with the migrating group maintaining some communication with its partner throughout reaction. It is certainly true that the vast majority of reactions that we will consider in this book will fall into this category. However, to adhere too rigidly to such an interpretation would exclude such reactions as allylic and Pummerer rearrangements, which result in a reorganisation of the original substrate by initial elimination of a group from the substrate, with subsequent attack by it, or another of the same species, at the new position. These reactions will be discussed in the final chapter.

Most rearrangements we will consider involve the migrating species bonding at the migration terminus through the same atom that was originally bonded at the origin. However, we will not ignore migrations involving anchimeric assistance, nor will we exclude sigmatropic rearrangements which proceed *via* charge separated precursors such as the Stevens rearrangement or the sulphoxide–sulphenate rearrangement .

Conversely, we will not include *prototropic* rearrangements—reactions which involve deprotonation–reprotonation sequences only. As a result, a large number of isomerisation reactions such as keto–enol and imine–

enamine tautomerism, which might quite justifiably be considered to be rearrangements, will not be dealt with here.

Therefore, our answer to the rhetorical question at the head of this section is: *This book will cover structural reorganisation processes involving the breaking and forming of σ- or π- bonds, in which some degree of charge separation is generated at the reacting sites prior to, or during, migration of a group, or an atom other than a proton, from one atom to another.*

Let us now consider briefly the various categories of rearrangement mechanism and decide which are likely to involve polar intermediates.

Heterolytic rearrangements

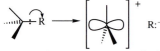

In heterolytic bond cleavage both bonding electrons become associated with one fragment. Movement of a pair of electrons is shown by a 'curly arrow'.
A *nucleophile* attacks centres of positive charge. An *electrophile* reacts with centres of negative charge.

In such stepwise reactions, initial fragmentation gives rise to a positively or negatively charged species which can undergo rearrangement. In the first instance, the migrating group retains the electrons (*nucleophilic or anionotropic rearrangement*); whereas in the second case it gives up its electrons (*electrophilic or cationotropic rearrangement*). Nucleophilic rearrangements are encountered far more commonly than electrophilic rearrangements.

 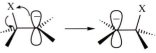

Nucleophilic rearrangement   Electrophilic rearrangement

Homolytic rearrangements

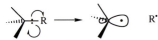

In homolytic bond cleavage one bonding electron becomes associated with each fragment. Note the use of 'curly fish hooks' to denote the movement of single electrons.

These reactions are also stepwise, with initial bond cleavage taking place to produce a radical species possessing an unpaired electron prior to migration.

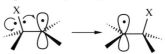

By their very nature, such rearrangements are usually non–polar, but there are some which involve charged radical intermediates as the reacting species. For instance, the Hofmann–Loffler–Freytag reaction involves an intramolecular hydrogen atom abstraction by a nitrogen radical cation:

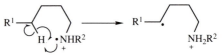

Pericyclic rearrangements

These single step rearrangements do not involve the formation of recognisable intermediates and were once referred to as 'no mechanism reactions', although they actually fall into the categories of pericyclic reactions known as *electrocyclic* and *sigmatropic rearrangements*. Pericyclic rearrangements do not proceed *via* any intermediates but pass through highly ordered transition states. As such they are relatively insensitive to external influences and are generally very non-polar in nature.

The Claisen and Cope rearrangements, in which one three-carbon fragment migrates across another three-carbon fragment, are typical examples of molecular rearrangements and are termed 3,3-sigmatropic rearrangements.

Note that the the chair is the preferred conformation for the transition state in 3,3-sigmatropic rearrangements.

The Claisen rearrangement (X = O) and Cope rearrangement (X = CH_2).

Although typically non-polar, some molecular rearrangements, such as the 2,3-sigmatropic rearrangement of an allylic sulphur ylid to a homoallylic sulphide, involve substrates in which charge separation in the substrate plays a necessary role.

Others, for instance Lewis acid catalysed variants of the Claisen rearrangement, involve charged reactive species. How much such reactions have ceased to be truly concerted, and have developed some step-wise character is a matter for debate.

From this brief introduction it should be fairly clear that the bulk of 'polar rearrangements' considered in this book will be those reactions which fall into the category of heterolytic rearrangements and these will be discussed first. However, it is useful to consider some of the general mechanistic and theoretical aspects of these reactions before looking at specific examples.

1.2 Heterolytic rearrangements: sub-classification

Migrations to electron deficient carbon

Nucleophilic rearrangements occur when an electron deficient site is generated close to a group capable of migrating using either a lone pair or a bonding pair of electrons. The commonest situation occurs when the *migration origin* and the *migration terminus* are on adjacent atoms with the migrating species being either a hydride or an alkyl group, and these processes are referred to as *1,2-hydride shifts* (so called because one atom moves across two atoms) or *1,2-alkyl shifts*, respectively.

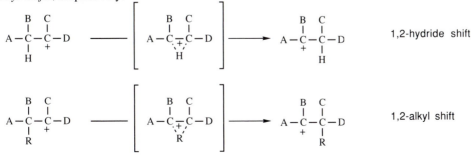

1,2-hydride shift

1,2-alkyl shift

Many nucleophilic rearrangements, often grouped under the heading of *Wagner–Meerwein shifts*, occur by the 1,2-migration of an alkyl group to a carbocationic centre. The different variants of this reaction will be considered individually in Chapter 2 but, while they may differ in the way that the initial carbocation is generated or the way that the product carbocation is quenched, they all follow the same overall mechanistic pathway. Almost invariably the main driving force for such rearrangements is the formation of a more stable (usually more substituted) carbocation, perhaps with some associated relief from steric compression.

The rearrangement sequence may then be terminated either by reaction with a nucleophile or by loss of a positively charged species, such as a proton, to regenerate the neutral rearrangement product. The following reaction of neopentyl iodide with silver nitrate exemplifies these features; neopentylic systems are renowned for their readiness to undergo rearrangements and reluctance to undergo direct S_N1 or S_N2 reactions of the leaving group.

The stability of carbocations is benzylic, allylic > 3° > 2° > 1°.

S_N1 : First order nucleophilic substitution
S_N2 : Second order nucleophilic substitution

S_N1 reaction of neopentylic substrates is disfavoured as formation of a 1° carbocation is necessary. S_N2 reaction is sterically disfavoured due to the presence of alkyl groups β- to the centre undergoing substitution.

E1: First order elimination

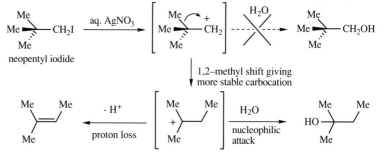

As this scheme demonstrates, one way of initiating such nucleophilic migrations involves loss of a good leaving group in exactly the same way as in the initial rate determining step of S_N1 and E1 reactions. In fact rearrangements often compete with such processes, and may dominate if the carbon adjacent to the initial carbocation is highly substituted such as in neopentylic systems.

It is extremely doubtful whether alkyl groups are capable of undergoing migrations over greater distances than between neighbouring atoms. One convincing piece of evidence to support this view is the fact that the 3,3-dimethyl-1-butyl cation only undergoes 1,2-hydride shift with no evidence for 1,3-methyl shift, despite the fact that this would furnish a much more stable carbocation.

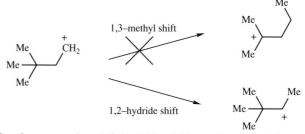

Likewise it seems that 1,3-hydride shifts only occur if very special geometric requirements are met and many apparent 1,3-hydride shifts actually turn out to be two successive 1,2-hydride shifts.

Migrations to electron deficient nitrogen

This category of very closely related reactions which occur *via* 1,2-alkyl shifts induced by the generation of a *nitrene* represents a very important class of reaction from the viewpoint of synthetic utility. A nitrene is a neutral, electron deficient species in which the nitrogen possesses only a sextet of electrons in its outer shell instead of the usual octet. One means of generating a nitrene is *via* decomposition of an azide, frequently an acyl azide, but we will consider other important precursors in Chapter 4.

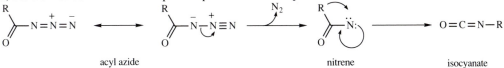

acyl azide   nitrene   isocyanate

The related Hofmann rearrangement probably occurs *via* a concerted mechanism without forming the intermediate nitrene.

Another important reaction in this series is the Beckmann rearrangement of oximes in which concerted stereoselective migration of the alkyl group *anti* to the hydroxyl group is a key feature.

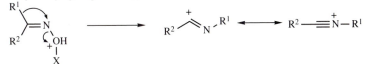

The common fate of the initial migration products involves nucleophilic addition of the hydroxylic solvent in which such rearrangements are usually carried out.

Migrations to electron deficient oxygen

This small group of reactions consisting of the Baeyer–Villiger rearrangement and hydroperoxide rearrangements, in which heterolytic cleavage of a peroxide O–O bond occurs in concert with an alkyl group migration, parallels carbon-to-nitrogen rearrangements. The leaving group is commonly a carboxylic acid or its conjugate base.

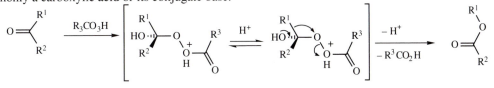

The Baeyer–Villiger rearrangement converts ketones to esters.

The concerted alkyl migration avoids the formation of what would be a highly unstable positively charged oxygen species, but you should note that these migration reactions are at variance with the standard reactivity of the peroxide linkage which usually undergoes homolytic cleavage. An interesting mechanistic feature of the Baeyer–Villiger rearrangement is that unsymmetrical ketones show highly selective migration of only one of the groups. The rule is that the group which is more highly substituted at the α-position to the carbonyl group is the one which migrates.

Other nucleophilic migrations

So far our criterion of classification has been based upon the nature of the migration terminus, assuming the migration origin to be a carbon atom. However boron as well as a wide range of transition metals can act as migration origins for nucleophilic migrations of alkyl and acyl groups and some of these reactions will be discussed in the final chapter.

Transannular hydride migrations

Despite the extreme reluctance towards migration over more than two atoms in *acyclic* systems, hydride migrations are possible over several carbons if the migration origin and the carbocation at the terminus are in close proximity. This situation can occur in medium ring systems (8-12 carbon atoms) when 1,4-, 1,5-, and 1,6-transannular hydride shifts are possible. Notice in the example shown here that the methyl group does not migrate. It is generally the case that such transannular rearrangements are not demonstrated by alkyl groups and only in special instances have aromatic groups been shown to migrate over these distances.

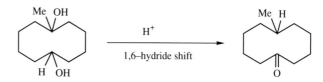

Electrophilic migrations

These less frequently encountered heterolytic migrations commonly involve the migration of an alkyl group from a heteroatom such as nitrogen, oxygen, and sulphur to a carbanionic centre. The Stevens rearrangement of tetra-alkylammonium salts and the Wittig rearrangement of ethers are examples of such rearrangements which have synthetic utility.

$$R^1CH_2\overset{+}{-}N(R^2)_3 \xrightarrow{\text{base}} \left[R^1\overset{-}{C}H\overset{+}{-}N(R^2)_3 \right] \longrightarrow \overset{R^1}{\underset{R'}{\diagdown}}CH-N(R^2)_2$$

A concerted electrophilic rearrangement is a four-electron process and orbital symmetry requirements dictate that this should take place with stereochemical inversion at the migrating carbon centre under thermal conditions. Studies on the mechanism of the Stevens rearrangement have shown it to be intramolecular, with the migrating centre retaining its stereochemistry. Such observations therefore rule out a concerted process and migration is now believed to proceed *via* initial homolytic fragmentation to yield a pair of radicals which remain in close contact with each other within a solvent cage. Recombination to form the rearranged product must be rapid to account for the absence of racemisation in the migrating group.

$$R^1CH_2-N(R^2)_3 \xrightarrow{\text{base}} R^1\overset{-}{C}H-\overset{+}{N}(R^2)_3 \longrightarrow \left[\begin{array}{c} R^1\overset{-}{C}H-\overset{+}{N}(R^2)_2 \\ \underset{R^2\bullet}{\bullet} \end{array} \longleftrightarrow \begin{array}{c} R^1CH-N(R^2)_2 \\ \underset{R^2\bullet}{\bullet} \end{array} \right] \longrightarrow \underset{R^2}{\overset{R^1}{\diagdown}}CH-N(R^2)_2$$

A similar mechanism is envisaged to operate for the sulphur ylid and Wittig rearrangements, although of course in the Wittig rearrangement homolytic cleavage furnishes a radical and a radical anion.

$$R^1CH_2-OR^2 \xrightarrow{\text{base}} R^1\overset{-}{C}H-OR^2 \longrightarrow \left[\begin{array}{c} R^1\overset{-}{C}H-O \\ \underset{R^2\bullet}{\bullet} \end{array} \longleftrightarrow \begin{array}{c} R^1CH-O^- \\ \underset{R^2\bullet}{\bullet} \end{array} \right] \longrightarrow \underset{R^2}{\overset{R^1}{\diagdown}}CH-O^-$$

Some electrophilic aryl migrations are known; for instance it has been demonstrated that Ph_3CCH_2Cl produces some Ph_2CHCH_2Ph on treatment with metallic sodium.

1.3 Mechanistic aspects of nucleophilic migrations

Nature of the rearrangement

There can be much variability in the timing of the steps of nucleophilic rearrangements between true stepwise generation of the carbocation followed by migration, and migration occurring in concert with the initial ionisation. These two situations can be considered as intramolecular analogues of S_N1 and S_N2 reactions, respectively.

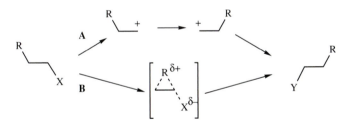

A Stepwise ionisation–migration.
B Concerted migration with charge separation.

This can have profound stereochemical implications at both the migration origin and the migration terminus; although this is only detectable when both centres are chiral and if the migration origin is not converted to an sp^2 centre by subsequent elimination of the rearranged cation. With non-racemic substrates the generation of a *free carbocation* at either the migration terminus or origin will result in loss of stereochemcal integrity at that centre; whereas a *concerted migration* with no intermediate will result in *inversion* of the absolute stereochemistry at the migration terminus.

Thus, in the following diagram depicting a generalised stepwise mechanism, the single enantiomer of the substrate gives rise to all possible diastereoisomeric rearrangement products. This is a result of the possibility of free rotation in the intermediates and planarity of the carbocations.

Free carbocations are planar and hence may be attacked by nucleophiles from either face leading to enantiomeric products.

The inversion in S_N2 substitution reactions is a consequence of the backside attack of the nucleophile upon the substrate.

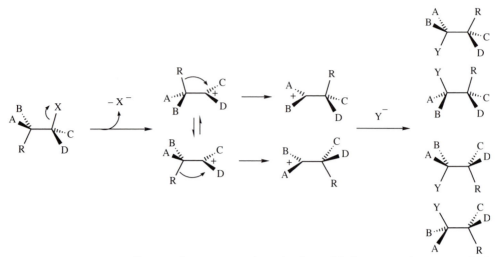

Conversely, a concerted mechanism with the same substrate would furnish only one enantiomer. In this case, the migrating group R must be positioned antiperiplanar to the leaving group X and is undergoing *neighbouring group participation* (also termed *anchimeric assistance*). We will consider neighbouring group effects in a later sub-section.

Two groups *antiperiplanar* to each other subtend a torsional angle of 180°. This is also known as a 'staggered' conformation.

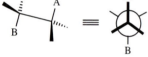

'saw-horse'   Newman
projection   projection

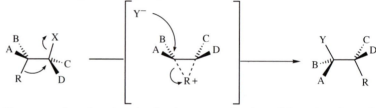

One case of a migration that leads to racemisation of the migration origin is the pinacol rearrangement of (S)-2-methylbutan-1,2-diol which forms racemic 2-methylbutanal.

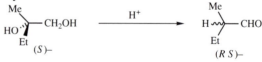

Whitmore has demonstrated inversion at the terminus during the pinacol type deamination of (−)-1,1-diphenyl-2-aminopropanol and Cram showed inversion at the origin and terminus in 3-phenyl-2-toluensulphonyloxy butanes (but more of this later).

A Stereochemical inversion at the migration terminus.   B Stereochemical inversion at the migration origin.

As we have already seen on page 5, one important example of the stereochemical consequence of concerted migration with loss of the leaving group occurs in the Beckmann rearrangement (Chapter 4) when it is the group *anti* to the hydroxyl group of the oxime which migrates.

Both alkyl groups of the oxime are necessarily coplanar due to the double bond.

Unfortunately, due to the configurational lability of oximes under acidic conditions, any stereochemical information is frequently masked by isomerisation prior to migration, but (*E*)-4-bromophenyl methyl ketoxime is one substrate which demonstrates this stereospecificity.

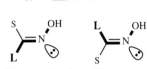

(*E*)- or *anti*-oxime   (*Z*)- or *syn*-oxime
(*E*)- and (*Z*)- nomenclature for describing alkene geometry may also be applied to oximes, the nitrogen lone pair being the fourth, lowest priority substituent (also referred to as *anti* and *syn* respectively).

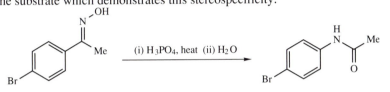

(i) H_3PO_4, heat   (ii) H_2O

Nature of the migrating species

Having considered what goes on at the migration sites, let us now turn our attention to the migrating group itself. In nucleophilic 1,2-shifts the migrating group remains co-ordinated to some degree with the substrate throughout the reaction. Crossover experiments, in which no exchange is observed, confirm the intramolecularity of the rearrangements. Even stronger evidence for how closely the two partners are associated during rearrangement can be obtained from the use of chiral migrating groups. Studies on Baeyer–Villiger, pinacol, Curtius, and Wagner–Meerwein rearrangements have confirmed that the migrating group always *retains* its absolute configuration. For example, in the case of 3-(*S*)-2,2,3-trimethylaminopentane, deaminative rearrangement furnished the alcohol with 98% retention of the chiral centre.

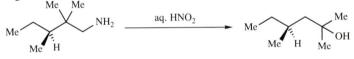

aq. HNO_2

Migratory aptitude

The ease with which any particular group will undergo nucleophilic 1,2-shift is known as its *migratory aptitude*. Although related to electron donating capacity, such values are not quantifiable as a single group will show different migratory aptitudes for different reactions or even for the same reaction under different conditions. Nevertheless, some general ranking system for different alkyl and aryl groups is very useful for predicting the outcome in situations where two different groups might undergo migration.

There are two ways in which relative migratory aptitudes may be determined. One way involves the comparison of relative rates of rearrangement in a homologous series of substrates, each possessing just one type of migrating group, under exactly the same reaction conditions. An alternative method analyses the product mixtures obtained from a substrate containing two different competing substituents at the migrating origin.

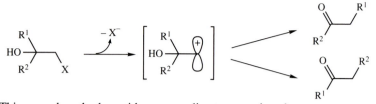

This second method provides a more direct comparison between two groups but, of course cannot be applied in all instances. In the Beckmann rearrangement for example, only the group *anti* to the oxime hydroxyl substituent migrates regardless of relative migratory aptitude of the two substituents. Similarly this technique cannot be applied to study relative migratory aptitudes in unsymmetrical pinacol substrates when formation of the most stable cation controls the reaction pathway. We have already seen one case of such control in the preferential migration of hydride over methyl or ethyl in the pinacol rearrangement of (*S*)-2-methylbutan-1,2-diol on page 8. In the following example, migration of the methyl group is determined by initial formation of the more stabilised carbocation rather than by a higher migratory aptitude of methyl over phenyl.

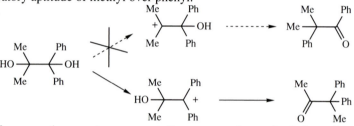

Of course, the way to carry out direct comparison of relative migratory aptitudes of methyl *versus* phenyl in the pinacol rearrangement is to use 2,3-diphenylbutane-2,3-diol as loss of either hydroxyl group generates the same carbocation.

A wide range of other factors, such as steric and conformational effects, play subtle roles in determining whether a particular migration is favoured or not and so it is not surprising that hard and fast predictions cannot be made. Generally aryl groups migrate more readily than alkyl groups, and within the aryl series, electron donating substituents increase the propensity for migration. However, the position of hydrogen within this framework is highly unpredictable. The following are some relative migratory aptitudes for pinacol rearrangement of various aromatic substituents:

Substrate for the direct comparison of Me *versus* Ph migration.

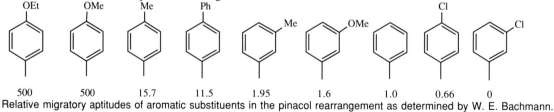

Relative migratory aptitudes of aromatic substituents in the pinacol rearrangement as determined by W. E. Bachmann.

Neighbouring group participation (anchimeric assistance)

When a substituent is capable of stabilising an adjacent carbocation by acting as an intramolecular nucleophile it is said to be undergoing *neighbouring group participation*. Winstein coined the term *anchimeric assistance* to indicate the fact that such reactions occur more readily than would be expected without this participation and the two terms are now effectively interchangeable.

Any β-substituent possessing an unshared electron pair or a double bond is a prime candidate for participation in this way as the effective concentration of the group is very high (it is adjacent to the cationic site) and relatively little molecular reorganisation is necessary to achieve the transition state. These two factors overcome the disadvantage of increased strain involved in formation of the bridged transition states.

σ–Participation in concerted 1,2–nucleophilic migration.

We have already noted (page 7) that concerted migration of a group with loss of a leaving group, in a process akin to an intramolecular S_N2 reaction, constitutes one example of neighbouring group participation. This type of interaction is sometimes referred to as *σ-participation* as it is the electrons of a σ-bond which are stabilising the developing electron deficiency at the adjacent site. Such participation can be detected by the resulting stereochemical inversion of the migration termini, and it turns out to be rare in open chain or unstrained cyclic compounds if the carbocation is generated at a secondary or tertiary centre and the migrating group is hydride or alkyl. The lack of neighbouring group participation in the pinacol rearrangement has been neatly demonstrated by allowing partial reaction of unlabelled pinacol in acidic ^{18}O labelled water and finding that unreacted pinacol had incorporated ^{18}O label. This observation is totally consistent with the generation of a free carbocation which either rearranges or adds water again and is inconsistent with a concerted migration process.

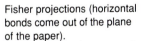

Such σ-participation by alkyl groups is known to occur in strained ring systems however, and will be considered later in the next sub-section on 'non-classical carbonium ions'. Neighbouring group participation is very favourable if the adjacent substituent has lone pairs available for donation, and is commonly encountered when oxygen, nitrogen or halogen containing functional groups such as the following are present:

$$R\overset{O}{\overset{\|}{C}}O-,\quad R\overset{O}{\overset{\|}{O}}C-,\quad Ar\overset{O}{\overset{\|}{C}}-,\quad RO-,\quad HO-,\quad H_2N-,\quad R_2N-,\quad HS-,\quad RS-,\quad I-,\quad Br-,\quad (Cl-)$$

One of the earliest pieces of evidence for neighbouring group participation came from the demonstration by Winstein that the two different diastereoisomers of 3-bromobutan-2-ol behaved differently in their reaction with HBr. The optically active *threo*-diastereoisomer was converted to a racemic mixture of the *threo*-dibromides whereas the optically active *erythro*-diastereoisomer cleanly gave the *meso*-dibromide. This showed that substitution of the hydroxyl group had occurred with retention of the original relative stereochemistry in both instances. These observations strongly

Fisher projections (horizontal bonds come out of the plane of the paper).

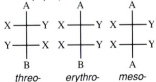

threo-   *erythro-*   *meso-*

Meso- compounds have a plane of symmetry and therefore cannot exhibit optical activity.

support the intervention of the adjacent bromine atom in the departure of the protonated hydroxyl group to form an intermediate *bromonium ion.*

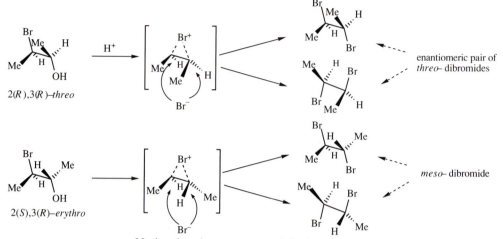

enantiomeric pair of *threo-* dibromides

meso- dibromide

Notice that the symmetry of the bromonium ion intermediates means that there is the possibility of nucleophilic attack by bromide at either C-2, to which the hydroxyl group was attached, or C-3, to which the bromine was originally attached. It is this feature that leads to racemisation in the *threo-*series and, in the case of bromide attacking C-3, the bromine originally present undergoes 1,2-shift.

Similar experiments by Cram have led to acceptance of the existence of the *phenonium ion.* Solvolysis of the optically active *threo-*diastereoisomers of the tosylate esters of 3-phenylbutan-2-ol in acetic acid resulted in the formation of racemic *threo-* acetates; whereas similar reaction of the optically active *erythro-*diastereoisomer furnished the optically active *erythro-*acetate.

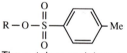

The *p*–toluenesulphonate (tosylate) group (⁻OTs) is a good leaving group.

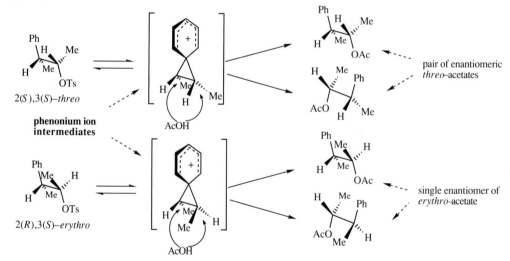

pair of enantiomeric *threo-*acetates

single enantiomer of *erythro-*acetate

Further evidence was obtained by isolating the starting material before complete reaction and finding that the *threo-*tosylate was almost totally racemised whereas the *erythro-*tosylate had retained its optical activity. These results indicate that the intermediate phenonium ions can either revert to starting materials or be attacked by acetic acid and go on to form substitution products. However, the phenonium ion derived from the *threo*-precursor which possesses a plane of symmetry bisecting the bond joining the two stereogenic centres (the so-called *meso*-configuration) is optically inactive, and hence gives rise to racemic starting material.

The formation of a phenonium intermediate may be envisaged as being equivalent to an intramolecular electrophilic substitution reaction and, by analogy, electron rich aryl groups might be expected to participate more readily. This expectation was indeed borne out by experimental observation of the effect of varying the aryl group in a series of brosylate (a slightly better leaving group than tosylate) esters of *threo*-3-arylbutan-2-ols upon reaction rate and product distribution. Whilst some of the products obtained were due to direct nucleophilic displacement of the leaving group by solvent, a good correlation between electron density of the aryl ring and propensity to undergo neighbouring group participation was observed, with the *p*-methoxyphenyl derivative reacting some 500 times faster than the phenyl derivative.

The symmetrically bridged structure of the phenonium ion has been demonstrated by ^{13}C n.m.r. spectroscopic analysis of the parent ion which may be generated in super-acid media. The studies showed that the bridging ring carbon had a chemical shift typical of a tetrahedral centre and the remaining ring carbons had chemical shifts comparable to benzenonium ions.

Non-classical carbonium ions

While alkyl groups do not usually undergo σ-participation in acyclic or unstrained ring systems, there is much evidence to suggest that this does occur in strained rings. The species formed contain a two-electron, three-centre bond and are known as '*non-classical carbonium ions*', although in the correct terminology they are simply *carbonium ions*. Unfortunately this nomenclature causes much confusion, since organic chemists are accustomed to the incorrect use of the term *carbonium ion* to describe species of the form R_3C^+ which are correctly termed *carbenium ions* or simply *carbocations*. To put the matter straight once and for all; a carbenium ion only contains two-electron, two-centre bonds; whereas a carbonium ion contains a two-electron, three-centre bond and the cationic centre has a coordination number of five.

The most studied system in which σ-participation is envisaged to occur is the 2-norbornyl system. Winstein found that solvolysis of optically pure norbornyl 2-*exo*-brosylate in acetic acid gave a racemic *exo*-acetate as the sole product with no *endo*-material. Furthermore, this solvolysis occurred 350 times faster than the optically active 2-*endo*-isomer which also furnished solely *exo*-material but this time with between 3 and 13% retention at the 2-position depending upon solvent.

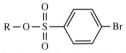

A *p*–bromophenylsulphonate (brosylate) ester (ROBs).

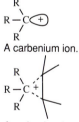

phenonium ion   **benzenonium ion**

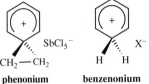

A carbenium ion.

A carbonium ion.

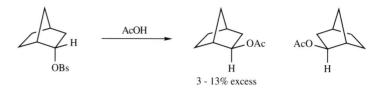

These results were interpreted as implying that the reaction of the *exo*-substrate occurred solely *via* a non-classical carbonium ion; whilst the *endo*-substrate reacted by initial formation of a classical carbenium ion which then rearranged to the non-classical carbonium ion, but not before a small amount had reacted with solvent, attack being sterically directed to the *exo*-face.

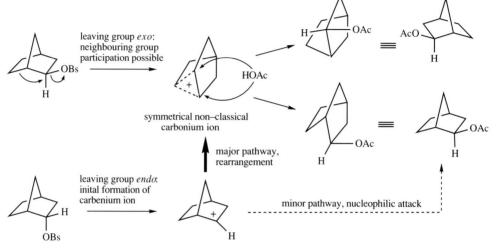

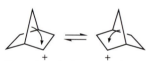

Brown's 'windscreen wiper' proposal.

This claim and others like it were hotly contested at the time by Brown who made the point that the results could equally well be explained by invoking an extremely rapidly interconverting pair of classical carbenium ions coupled with the established propensity for norbornyl systems to be attacked from the sterically more accessible *exo*-face. Nucleophilic attack at a rate much slower than the interconversion of the two carbenium ions would lead to the observed racemisation. Brown's hypothesis concluded that the rate of solvolysis of the *exo*-brosylate was not enhanced by neighbouring group participation but that the solvolysis of the *endo*-brosylate was retarded due to steric reasons.

The experimentally rigorous distinction between a non-classical carbonium ion and a pair of very rapidly interconverting carbenium ions is extremely difficult. Possibly some of the best evidence for the existence of such species comes from Olah's n.m.r. studies in super-acid media at low temperatures. The 2-norbornyl cation was shown to exhibit the symmetry properties expected of a non-classical species which could not be frozen out; whereas the the 2-phenylnorbornyl cation showed essentially classical behaviour.

Another system which has attracted much interest is that of the cyclopropylmethyl cation for similar reasons to the 2-norbornyl system: namely the great ease of solvolysis of cyclopropylmethyl substrates accompanied by formation of rearrangement products. Of particular interest is that, regardless of the method of generation of the cationic species, the ratio of products is always very similar. Both hydrolysis of cyclopropylmethyl chloride under conditions favouring S_N1 substitution and diazotisation of cyclopropylamine produce cyclobutanol and but-3-en-1-ol as well as cyclopropylmethanol in approximately 47%, 5%, and 48% yields respectively. Moreover, diazotisation of cyclobutylamine also produces the same three alcohols in the same ratios.

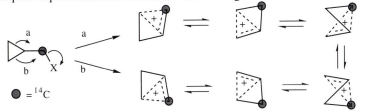

Additional information is obtained from studies using $1\text{-}^{14}C$ labelled cyclopropylmethylamine which show much (but not total) scrambling of the label over all of the methylene carbons in the products.

So far the data might be interpreted by invoking a set of very rapidly interconverting classical carbocations, but difference in rates of solvolysis of cyclopropylmethyl derivatives compared with the corresponding 2-methyl-1-propyl derivatives ($10^6 : 1$) appears to demand σ-participation. The scheme involving the formation of non-classical *bicyclobutonium ions* proposed by Roberts is generally accepted to explain all the features of this system. This envisages the initial formation of two equivalent three-centre carbonium ions by methylene assisted loss of the leaving group, followed by equilibration of these structures through a whole array of equivalent intermediates. These subsequent equilibria result in ultimate scrambling of the carbon atoms.

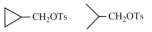

Cyclopropylmethyl tosylate solvolyses one million times faster than 2-methylprop-1-yl tosylate.

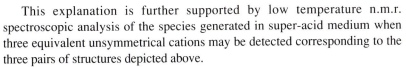

Generation of cyclobutonium ions by neighbouring group participation of either adjacent methylene group is followed by equilibration. Note that all of the ions are in equilibrium with each other but the remaining arrows have been omitted for clarity.

This explanation is further supported by low temperature n.m.r. spectroscopic analysis of the species generated in super-acid medium when three equivalent unsymmetrical cations may be detected corresponding to the three pairs of structures depicted above.

1.4 Summary

In this first chapter we have surveyed the sorts of reactions that we will be considering in further detail in the remainder of this book. In addition, mechanistic aspects of the most important class of polar rearrangements—nucleophilic rearrangements—have been discussed. This treatment has of necessity been superficial and those requiring more information should consult some of the references given at the end of this chapter. However, the rest of the book will assume that you understand the basic aspects presented here and you may find it useful to refer back to this introductory chapter as you read through the book.

1.5 Exercises

1.   The treatment of 3-amino-2,3-dimethyl-2-butanol with nitrous acid, 3-chloro-2,3-dimethyl-2-butanol with aqueous silver nitrate, and 2,3-epoxy-2,3-dimethylbutane with aqueous hydrochloric acid yield mixtures of a diol and a ketone in the same proportions in each instance (although the reactions proceed at different rates). Suggest structures for these two products and propose a mechanism which is consistent with the observations.

2. For the following diols predict the major rearrangement product formed on treatment with cold dilute acid and say in each case whether the pathway is a consequence of relative stability of intermediate cations or relative migratory aptitudes of the migrating groups:

(i)   2,3-diphenylbutan-2,3-diol
(ii)   1,1-diphenyl-2-methylpropan-1,2-diol
(iii)   2-methylpropan-1,2-diol
(iv)   butan-2,3-diol

3.   Caprolactam is an important industrial chemical for which one possible precursor is cyclohexanone. Describe a synthetic route that might be applicable to commercial conversion of cyclohexanone into caprolactam.

caprolactam

4.   Suggest the likely products of the following reactions:

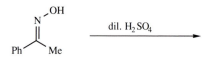

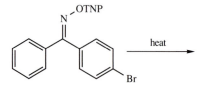

(TNP = 2,4,6–trinitrophenyl)

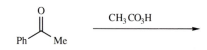

5.   Benzophenone oxime, on heating in acid, is transformed into a solid (**1**) which is insoluble in dilute aqueous acid or base. However, on prolonged heating with aqueous base, (**1**) reacts to give an oil (**2**) which may be purified by steam distillation. Acidification of the aqueous residue of the reaction causes precipitation of a solid (**3**). Compound (**2**) is soluble in dilute hydrochloric acid and, when this chilled solution is treated sequentially with sodium nitrite and 2-hydroxynaphthalene, a red precipitate is formed. Suggest a series of steps, giving mechanistic detail, to explain these observations and identify (**1**), (**2**), (**3**), and the red compound.

Further reading

General aspects of rearrangements: P. de Mayo (ed.), *Molecular Rearrangements*, Interscience, New York, 1963 (2 vols); S. Patai (ed.), *The Chemistry of the Carbonyl Group*, Interscience, New York, 1966, pp. 761–821.
Nucleophilic rearrangements see: G. W. Wheland, *Advanced Organic Chemistry*, 3rd edn, Wiley, New York, 1960, pp. 550–619.
Electrophilic rearrangements: D. J. Cram, *Fundamentals of Carbanion Chemistry*, Academic Press, New York, 1965, pp. 223–43.
Sigmatropic rearrangements see: C. W. Spangler, *Chem. Rev.*, 1976, **76**, 187. Another useful introduction to most of the reaction types that will be discussed in this book is the work of B. P. Mundy and M. G. Ellerd, *Name Reactions and Reagents in Organic Synthesis*, Wiley, New York, 1988.

2. Carbocation induced alkyl and hydride shifts

2.1 Wagner–Meerwein shifts and related reactions

During the latter part of the nineteenth century sufficient structural information had been amassed by early investigators into some of the components of 'essential oils' of plants to establish basic family likenesses. Many of these volatile, commonly fragrant, compounds were found to be unsaturated hydrocarbons or their oxygenated derivatives containing ten carbon atoms and were given the name *terpenes* or *terpenoids*. However, although the molecular formulae of these compounds could be obtained by combustion and cryoscopic analysis, attempts at deducing the carbon skeleta by degradative techniques frequently gave baffling results.

It was Georg Wagner in 1899 who made the first breakthrough of realising that the problems encountered by others were a consequence of the ease with which terpenes undergo skeletal reorganisations. The second key to the conceptual puzzle was provided by Hans Meerwein in 1922 (from studies on the camphene hydrochloride–isobornyl chloride interconversion) when he proposed that cationic species were involved. Later, in 1927, Meerwein generalised the carbocationic mechanism to account for other terpenic rearrangements and, in 1932, Frank Whitmore unified a series of apparently unrelated acyclic reactions, including the Hofmann, Curtius, Lossen, and Demjanov rearrangements, by stating that they involved the initial formation of electron deficient carbon centres.

Upon these proposals are laid the foundations for our understanding of nucleophilic rearrangements. With the benefit of hindsight it can be difficult to appreciate the fundamental value of the contributions of Wagner and Meerwein, but it is a fitting tribute to these two chemists that the archetypal nucleophilic rearrangement should be called after them. Although originally applied to 1,2-migration in bridged bicyclic molecules such as the camphenyl system, the term is now generally used for all nucleophilic 1,2-migrations of alkyl or aryl groups from carbon to carbon.

A common way of generating the intermediate carbocation involves loss of a good leaving group such as in protonation of a hydroxyl group and loss of water. Carbocations of this type may undergo direct elimination or substitution reactions depending upon the nucleophilic species present. However, *Wagner–Meerwein rearrangement* will occur if it leads to the new carbocation being more stabilised than the original. This is usually the case if the carbon adjacent to the positively charged centre is secondary or tertiary.

The word 'terpene' is derived from *turp*entine and alk*ene*.

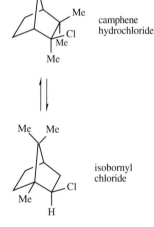

camphene hydrochloride

isobornyl chloride

The fate of the rearranged carbocation depends upon the structure of the molecule but commonly involves quenching by elimination or, less frequently, addition of a nucleophile. Alternatively, further rearrangement may occur to give a more stabilised carbocation and such cascade rearrangements are the basis of the biological construction of complex terpene molecules.

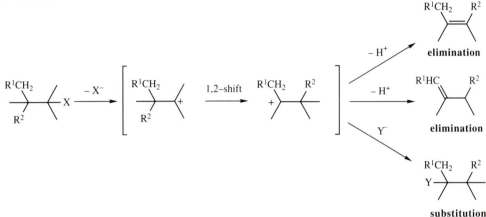

If there is a choice of protons which might be lost in an elimination, Saytzeff's rule is obeyed to give the most substituted alkene. In the first sequence shown below, rearrangement of the carbocation derived from isoborneol produces a new species for which there is no such choice (elimination in the alternative sense would produce an *anti-Bredt* bridgehead alkene) and, on elimination, forms camphene possessing an *exo*-methylene group. On the other hand, rearrangement of neopentyl chloride in the presence of aqueous base forms the most substituted alkene on deprotonation.

Saytzeff's rule states: 'In E1 elimination processes the most highly substituted alkene is formed.'

Bredt's rule states: 'Double bonds at a bridgehead are not possible for small ring systems.' (Not true if the ring containing the *trans*-double bond component is nine-membered or larger.)

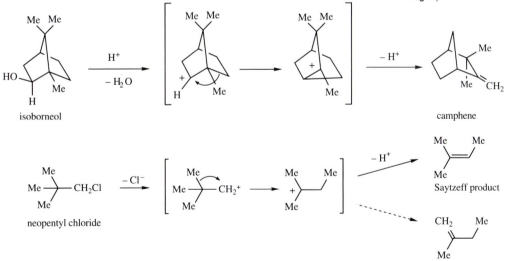

If the incoming nucleophile is the same as the initial leaving group the overall reaction is that of an isomerisation. We have already seen one such example in the ready equilibration of camphene hydrochloride with isobornyl chloride on dissolution in an inert solvent. Under kinetic conditions, Wagner–Meerwein rearrangements are directed *via* the stablest carbocationic intermediate but, in this case, the camphenyl system exists in equilibrium with the isobornyl system due to the higher propensity of camphene hydrochloride to ionise. In other words, the overall product distribution can be the result of a fine balance of kinetic and thermodynamic factors.

In particular, 1,2-alkyl shifts have a rigorous stereochemical requirement for the bond at the migration origin to lie very close to the plane of the vacant *p*-orbital of the carbocationic centre. Whilst acyclic systems can usually adopt the correct conformation for optimal alignment by rotation about single bonds, this option may not be open to cyclic systems—particularly those found in the terpenes. This requirement, coupled with the poorer relative migratory aptitude of the methyl group and the reluctance to form a four-membered ring in the case of migration of the tertiary substituent, are the factors which control the selective conversion of isoborneol into camphene.

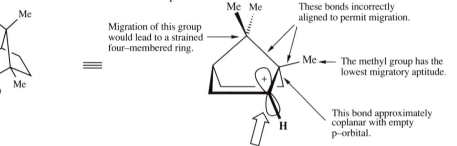

Migration of this group would lead to a strained four–membered ring.

These bonds incorrectly aligned to permit migration.

The methyl group has the lowest migratory aptitude.

This bond approximately coplanar with empty p–orbital.

Polycyclic systems provide some very good examples of rearrangements under thermodynamic control and this has been put to good synthetic use for the preparation of adamantane and its derivatives. Adamantane, possessing the structure of the repeating unit of the diamond lattice, is the stablest alkane of molecular formula $C_{10}H_{16}$ and all other isomeric tricyclic alkanes are converted to adamantane if subjected to sufficiently vigorous Lewis acid treatment. This situation is general and the stablest molecule of any set of isomeric alkanes (sometimes referred to as the *stabilomer*) will be formed by treatment with Lewis acid catalysts under equilibrating conditions.

A *Lewis acid* accepts electron pairs.
A *Brönsted acid* is a proton donor.

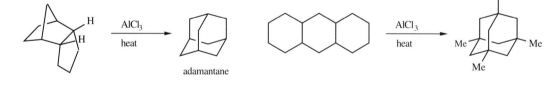

adamantane

Notice that, under these vigorous conditions, even alkanes can act as sources of the carbocationic species. Precursors suitable for promotion of Wagner–Meerwein shifts under relatively mild conditions are azides, halides, and alkenes, and we will look at examples of the use of these substrates later.

Hydride shifts can also occur in place of alkyl shifts if to do so would generate a more stable carbocation or if the alkyl migrations are not stereochemically favourable. In the 2-norbornyl system, a degenerate 1,2-

hydride shift of the *exo*-hydrogen at C-3 may occur in addition to alkyl migration.

1,2-Methyl shifts in terpenes: the Nametkin rearrangement

This particular type of Wagner–Meerwein shift has been singled out for special recognition due to its importance in the field of terpene chemistry. Single Nametkin rearrangements are often observed in monoterpenes during exposure to acid; for instance the conversion of α-methylcamphene to 4-methylisoborneol involves both a Nametkin and a Wagner–Meerwein rearrangement. (In this case notice that methyl migration competes successfully with the Wagner–Meerwein shift, unlike in the 2-bornyl cation considered earlier. This is presumably due to the fact that 4-methylisoborneol is the stablest product possible from the rearrangement sequences.)

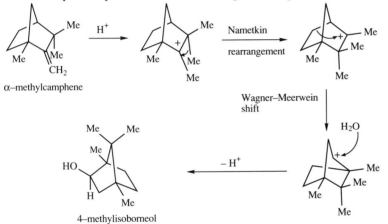

Nametkin rearrangements are commonly encountered in acid catalysed dehydrations of 3,3-dimethyl[2.2.1]bicycloheptan-2-ols such as in the camphenilol derivatives shown below and these can be seen to be further examples of rearrangements of neopentyl derivatives.

R = H; camphenilol
R = Me; 4-methylcamphenilol

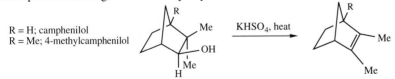

However, when it comes to examples of Nametkin rearrangements, the chemist has been comprehensively upstaged by Nature in the construction of polycyclic terpenes when cascades of 1,2-shifts can occur causing wholesale reorganisation of the carbon skeleton of the substrate molecule. All evidence points to the biological processes being essentially the same mechanistically (albeit enzyme mediated) as the acid catalysed rearrangements we have been

A *monoterpene* is a molecule composed of two C_5 subunits formally derived from isoprene.

isoprene

A *diterpene* is a molecule composed of four C_5 subunits, and a *triterpene* six C_5 subunits.

considering, and it is possible to emulate some of these processes *in vitro* with suitable substrates. The few examples shown here cannot do justice to the range and complexity of the types of cation initiated rearrangements that occur in living systems.

Steroids are *triterpenes* derived from a common acyclic C_{30} precursor squalene *via* oxidative multiple cyclisation initiated by acid catalysed ring opening of squalene epoxide. This forms initially a tetracyclic enzyme-bound intermediate which is ideally disposed to undergo a series of cation induced 1,2-hydride and 1,2-methyl shifts. In animals the process is terminated by deprotonation to form lanosterol which is the precursor to cholesterol and then on to the sex hormones, bile acids, and vitamin D.

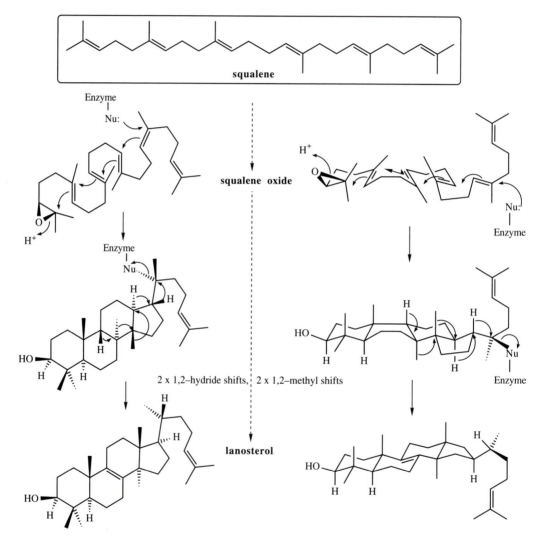

In plants and yeasts the new cationic intermediate is quenched by an enzyme bound nucleophile instead of undergoing proton loss as in the above sequence. This enzyme bound intermediate leads to the *phytosterols* (plant steroids) such as ergosterol in yeasts and sistosterol in higher plants.

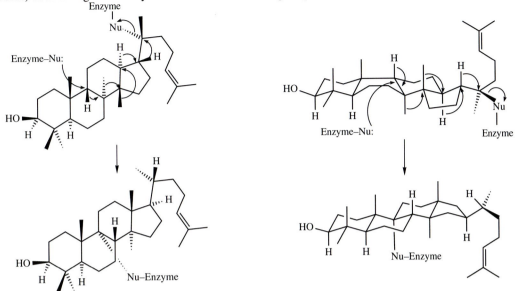

Notice that, as a consequence of the antiperiplanar stereochemistry of these migrations, the backbone of the tetracycle undergoes a fundamental and completely stereospecific reorganisation. The elimination and nucleophilic termination processes in these biological systems are exactly analogous to the fates of rearrangement products in non-biological systems.

The triterpene fern-9-ene, produced by the fern *polygodium vulgare*, is also derived from squalene *via* a non-oxidative, acid catalysed polycyclisation, followed by a cascade containing four 1,2-hydride shifts and two 1,2-methyl shifts. This series of shifts once again results in total rearrangement of the backbone of the molecule.

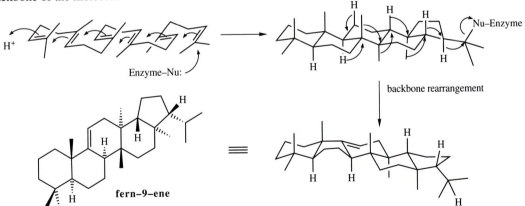

fern–9–ene

backbone rearrangement

That the stereospecificity of such migrations is dictated by the electronic requirements of the system and is not simply a result of enzyme control can be demonstrated in the laboratory by the acid catalysed cascade rearrangement of 3β-friedelanol. This gives 13(18)-oleanonene on treatment with acid *via* a stereospecific sequence of three 1,2-hydride shifts and four 1,2-methyl shifts.

In steroid stereochemical nomenclature substituents pointing out of the plane of the paper are designated β- and those pointing into the plane of the paper are designated α-.

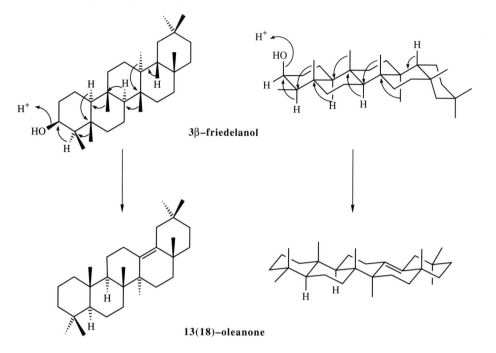

3β–friedelanol

13(18)–oleanone

One final example shows the configurational requirement for colinearity of the migrating group with the empty *p*-orbital of the Nametkin rearrangement. Of the two estradiols, epimeric at C-17, only the one possessing the 17α-hydroxyl group undergoes rearrangement.

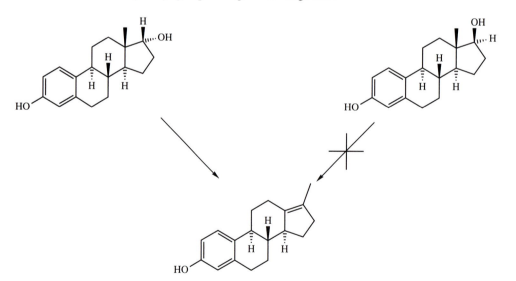

This requirement for an antiperiplanar relationship between the methyl group undergoing migration and the hydroxyl group which is lost is indicative of some degree of concertedness of migration occurring with loss of the leaving group.

2.2 The pinacol rearrangement

The *pinacol rearrangement* refers to the treatment of 1,2-diols with acid with subsequent conversion to carbonyl compounds. A variant of this reaction, sometimes known as the *semipinacol rearrangement* occurs with β-amino alcohols as substrates which, on diazotisation with nitrous acid, undergo similar transformation. In all instances, the major driving force for the rearrangement is the energetic advantage of generating a carbonyl group.

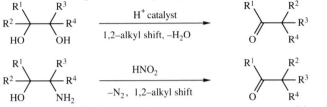

General pinacol rearrangement.

Semipinacol rearrangement of β-amino alcohols

Other substrates which show similar reactivity on treatment with acids or Lewis acids include epoxides, halohydrins, and allylic alcohols. Once again the initial intermediate is the carbocation in each case.

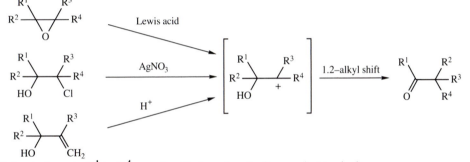

The diol substituents R^1 to R^4 may be alkyl, aryl or hydrogen, but typical pinacol rearrangement substrates are tetrasubstituted. The 1,2-diol precursors may be constructed by dihydroxylation of alkenes or by reductive coupling of ketones, the latter reaction only being of practical value for the preparation of symmetrical diols. The different ways of converting an alkene to a 1,2-diol permit greater flexibility, particularly in the stereochemistry of addition to the double bond and alkenes are usually the substrates of choice for the preparation of such systems (OsO$_4$ and KMnO$_4$ give *syn*-dihydroxylation; whereas peracid epoxidation followed by cleavage, or I$_2$–RCO$_2$Ag followed by hydrolysis, result in overall *anti*-dihydroxylation).

1,2–Diols are sometimes referred to as vic-*diols*, *glycols*, or if symmetrical, *pinacols*.

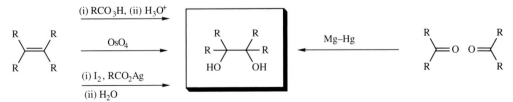

We have already seen that, with unsymmetrical substrates, the group migrating is largely determined by a combination of factors such as carbocation stability and relative migratory aptitudes of the substituents, but mixtures frequently result. Reaction conditions may also play a part in deciding which group migrates. For instance, the action of cold concentrated sulphuric acid upon 2-methyl-1,1-diphenylpropane-1,2-diol results in the formation of the kinetic product, the methyl group migrating as a consequence of the initial formation of the most favoured carbocation. Under conditions where equilibration may occur however, the product is the one in which the phenyl group migrates to give the most stable material, presumably due to lower steric encumbrance in the product.

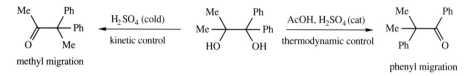

Aldehydes may be produced if substrates possessing either secondary or primary alcohol centres are rearranged under mild (kinetic) conditions. More rigorous conditions often result in further isomerisation of the aldehydic products to ketones.

The pinacol rearrangement is particularly useful for the generation of *spirocyclic* systems. For example, the two substrates shown below both give rise to the same spirobicyclic ketone on treatment with acid.

Spirocyclic molecules contain two rings possessing one common atom. The term is derived from the Latin 'spira' meaning pretzel.

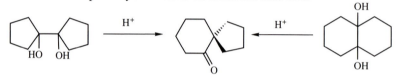

In these examples, the first diol could be readily obtained by reductive coupling of cyclopentanone; whereas the two diastereomeric decalindiols could be obtained by *syn-* or *anti*-alkene hydroxylation procedures.

2.3 The Tiffeneau–Demyanov reaction

We have already seen that β-amino alcohol derivatives undergo nucleophilic rearrangement on treatment with nitrous acid. In acyclic systems the reaction is often referred to as the *semipinacol rearrangement*. The difference between this and the pinacol rearrangement is that the carbocation is generated by diazotisation of an aliphatic amine, followed by loss of nitrogen, and not by protonation of an alcohol followed by water loss. The rearrangement of the carbocation once generated is the same as in the pinacol rearrangement.

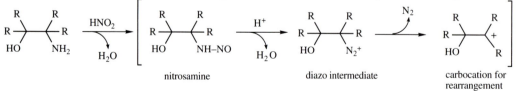

The required β-amino alcohol substrates possessing an aminomethylene moiety may be obtained directly by the reduction of α-amino acids, or from carbonyl compounds by conversion to cyanohydrins. Alternatively, Henry reaction of ketones with the α-anions of aliphatic nitro-compounds to generate β-nitroalcohols, followed by reduction, can be used to prepare a wide range of substrates.

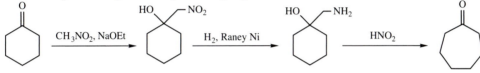

Nitro-compounds possessing α-hydrogens may be deprotonated. The anionic species is stabilised by resonance:

The addition of these anions to carbonyl compounds to generate nitroalcohols is known as the **Henry reaction.**

A specific variant of this reaction which leads to one carbon ring expansion is known as the *Tiffaneau–Demyanov reaction* and is very useful for homologating cyclic ketones to give products containing four to eight carbon atoms in the ring. Indeed, as the product is the homologated ketone, repetition of this procedure permits stepwise ring expansion if so desired.

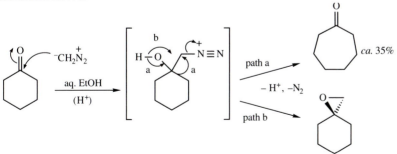

ca. 41% overall

An equivalent reaction can occur on treatment of cyclic ketones with diazomethane, the intermediate adduct undergoing ring expansion. The yields of this process are frequently lower than those obtained by the diazotisation of β-amino alcohols, as epoxides are sometimes formed as by-products. For this reason the best yields are usually obtained with strained ketones which more readily undergo skeletal rearrangement than their unstrained counterparts. The reaction works best in alcoholic solvents, presumably due to the hydroxylic solvent acting as a proton donor for the adduct. Although lower yielding, this one-step procedure is often convenient for the rapid preparation of small quantities of a particular ketone. The preparation of cycloheptanone by this procedure is shown here for comparison with that illustrated above.

Diazomethane has two extreme resonance structures (A and B). Drawing form A always makes it easier to explain the reactivity of this molecule.

$$\bar{C}H_2 - \overset{+}{N} \equiv N \longleftrightarrow CH_2 = \overset{+}{N} = \bar{N}$$
A   **B**

In the case of small ring ketones, the epoxide by-products can also be converted into ring expanded ketones by the action of mildly Lewis acidic reagents in yet another variant of the semipinacol rearrangement discussed earlier in this chapter. Although this requires formation of the less substituted carbocation in the first example shown, the driving force for the reaction is the loss of strain on expanding the small ring.

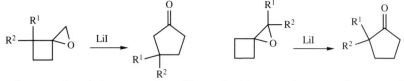

Base catalysed ring expansion of bromohydrins constitutes another way of carrying out this conversion.

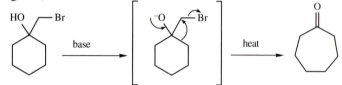

Whilst diazomethane is commonly the reagent used for this conversion due to the ease of its preparation, higher homologues may also be used in the Tiffaneau–Demyanov reaction.

2.4 The dienone–phenol and related rearrangements

Another way of generating carbocationic centres suitable for initiating migration involves protonation of the oxygen of a carbonyl group. This approach is particularly efficient in the case of 4,4-disubstituted cyclohexa-2,5-dienones as 1,2-migration of one of the substituents permits the new cationic species to be quenched by deprotonation resulting in an aromatic ring. The reaction is known as the *dienone–phenol rearrangement* after the substrates and products involved. Formally at least, the reaction can be considered to be a reverse of the pinacol rearrangement in which the disadvantage of losing a carbonyl group is overcome by the driving force of aromatisation.

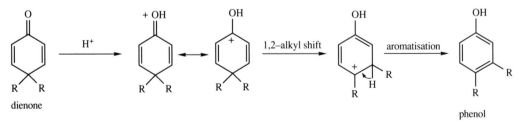

Rearrangements of aldehydes and ketones

Aldehydes possessing α-substituents may be converted to ketones on treatment with acid. The mechanism of the process has not been unambiguously elucidated and there is evidence that two pathways may operate in different circumstances. Ketones may also be interconverted but the conditions required are more vigorous and the products are possibly the thermodynamically most favoured. Due to the low migratory aptitude of hydride, the conversion of a ketone possessing α-hydrogens into an aldehyde has not been reported. One proposed mechanism (path a) involves two 1,2-alkyl shifts in opposite senses; whereas the alternative (path b) invokes two 1,2-alkyl shifts in the same direction, accompanied by a shift of the oxygen in the opposite direction. Labelling studies have been carried out which support the existence of both pathways in certain substrates. Note that in the second pathway, one of the intermediates is simply a protonated epoxide, and epoxides are known substrates for rearrangements of the semipinacol variety.

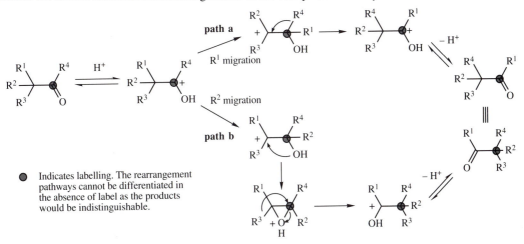

Indicates labelling. The rearrangement pathways cannot be differentiated in the absence of label as the products would be indistinguishable.

Rearrangement of ketones possessing α-oxygen or α-nitrogen substituents

Another way in which it is possible to use protonation of a carbonyl group to promote rearrangement is if the rearranged cation can itself furnish another carbonyl group. This is the case with α-ketol substrates which can be isomerised under acidic conditions. If the alcohol group of the ketol is tertiary then this rearrangement may also be initiated by base treatment but the mechanism is essentially the same.

Of couse, if the alkyl substituents are the same, the rearrangement becomes degenerate as the starting material and products have the same structure.

α-Amino ketones may undergo a similar rearrangement on heating to give products in which two substituents have switched positions. The mechanism involves initial protonation of the carbonyl oxygen, followed by 1,2-migration and quenching of the rearranged cation by loss of a proton from the amino substituent. An intramolecular proton transfer can be envisaged for this process but, although it is not possible to say if this actually does occur, the general mechanism is supported by the observation that fully substituted α–hydroxyimines also undergo this rearrangement

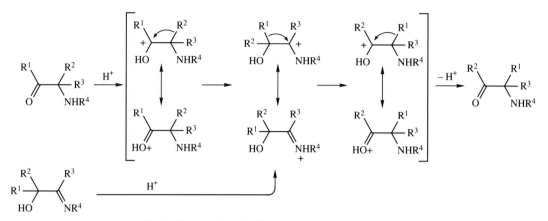

2.5 Hydride shifts

Just as alkyl groups may undergo 1,2-shifts, hydride is also a candidate for such rearrangements although, given the choice, it is usually the alkyl group which migrates as this normally results in the greatest steric relief. However, if steric requirements over-ride this control, 1,2-hydride shifts occur readily and we have seen several examples of multiple hydride shifts in the backbone rearrangements of steroids (pages 22–24).

Another system in which rapid 1,2-hydride migration may occur is the 2-norbornyl cation (pages 20, 21). In this case it is the well disposed *exo*-hydrogen at C-3 which migrates to the carbocation at C-2 and this has led to the rather confusing terminology of '*3,2-shift*' for this rearrangement. Although rapid, this rearrangement is degenerate and is normally overshadowed by the slower 1,2-alkyl shift typical of the isoborneol–camphene interconversion which accompanies the generation of such cations.

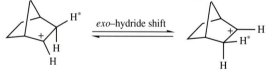

The inverse situation holds for the rearrangement of primary alkyl cations such as may be generated by the action of Lewis acids on 1-haloalkanes. In the freely rotating carbocation there is no steric bias for either alkyl or hydride shift but, whereas the alkyl shift is a degenerate process, hydride shift leads to a stable carbocation.

$$CH_3CH_2CH_2Br \xrightarrow{AlBr_3} \left[CH_3CH_2CH_2{}^+ \quad AlBr_4{}^- \xrightarrow{1,2-hydride\ shift} CH_3\overset{+}{C}HCH_3 \quad AlBr_4{}^- \right] \longrightarrow CH_3CHBrCH_3$$

Such migrations mean that Friedel–Crafts alkylations of aromatic substrates with haloalkanes usually furnish branched chain products irrespective of the position of the initially generated carbocation. This restricts further the use of Friedel–Crafts alkylation reactions which, in any event, tend to form mixtures of polyalkylated materials due to the activating inductive effect of an alkyl group on the aromatic nucleus.

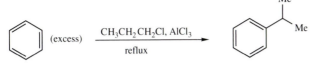

Transannular hydride migrations

Hydride migrations involving more than neighbouring centres in open chain substrates appear generally to be highly disfavoured and most 1,*n*-hydride shifts can be accounted for by a number of 1,2-hydride shifts occurring in series.

However, hydride rearrangements over large distances are well documented in medium ring (8–11 membered) carbocycles. In such cases, many of the ground state conformations available to medium rings bring opposing members of the ring into close proximity to each other permitting *transannular hydride migration* on generation of a carbocationic centre although alkyl groups do not undergo the same process.

small rings 3, 4 membered
normal rings 5–7 membered
medium rings 8 – 11 membered
large rings 12+ membered

'chair–boat' cyclooctane   'chair–boat–chair' cyclodecane

Representative conformations for cyclooctane and cyclodecane indicating the close approach of opposed hydrogens (all other hydrogens omitted for clarity).

Such shifts were first noted when the acid catalysed opening of medium ring epoxides was found to give only small amounts of the desired *trans*-1,2-diols. For example, cyclooctene epoxide gave a mixture of products consisting of *trans*-1,2-octanediol and *cis*-1,4-cycloctanediol as well as 3- and 4-cyclooctenols.

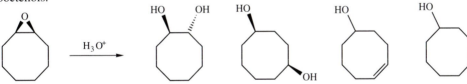

The 1,4-diol and cyclooctenols could arise by either 1,3- or 1,5-hydride shift and studies with 5,6-dideutero-1,2-epoxycyclooctane have shown that both occur, although 1,5-migration predominates. The formation of specifically *cis*-1,4-cyclooctanediol provides strong evidence for epoxide opening, hydride migration, and quenching of the carbocation occurring in a highly concerted manner, as a free carbocation would be expected to produce a stereorandom mixture of diols. However, kinetic isotope effect studies of the cyclooctyl system have given a value for k_H / k_D of 1.21 which is too small for significant cleavage of the C–H bond to be occurring in the rate determining step. Thus, the mechanism probably involves rate determining cleavage of the epoxide ring followed by rapid hydride migration with concommitant backside quenching of the developing carbocationic centre.

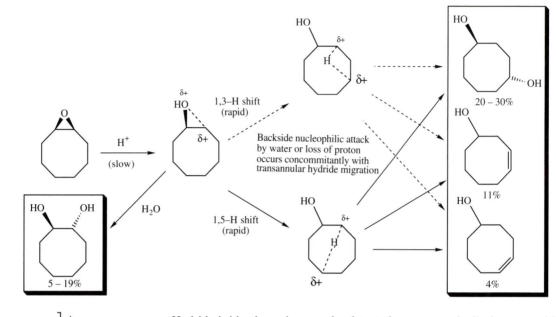

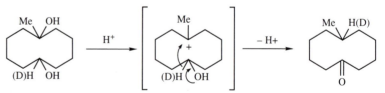

The cyclodecyl cation.

Hydride bridged species may be detected spectroscopically in superacid medium. The cyclodecyl cation in SbF_5–FSO_3H at –130 °C exhibits an extremely deshielded single proton at –6.85 δ whilst the ^{13}C n.m.r. spectrum shows the lowest field absorption at 152.8 δ integrating for two carbons. These data can be interpreted by invoking a bridged structure in which a hydride is shared between two centres.

A good example of the reluctance of alkyl groups to take part in such transannular migrations is provided by 1-methyl-1,6-cyclodecanediol which, on treatment with acid, rearranges to form 6–methylcyclodecanone with none of the alternative product resulting from methyl migration being detected. The fact that this was indeed a 1,6-hydride shift was clearly demonstrated by studying the substrate in which the carbinol proton had been replaced with a deuterium label.

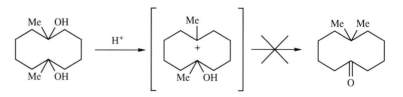

As further evidence of the reluctance of alkyl groups to undergo transannular shifts, 1,6-dimethyl-1,6-cyclodecanediol does not form any ketone on acid treatment.

2.6 Exercises

1. Upon dehydration with acid, 2,2-dimethylcyclohexanol forms two alkenes. Both result from rearrangement and one contains a five-membered ring. What are their structures?

2. Suggest structures for the rearrangement products formed on treatment of the following substrates with acid:

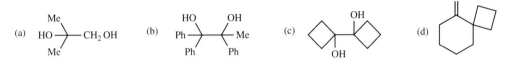

3. Suggest mechanisms for the reorganisation of the following terpenoid structures:

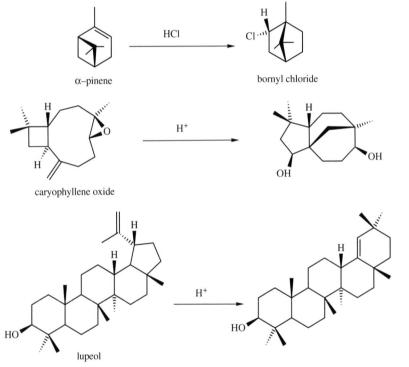

α–pinene

bornyl chloride

caryophyllene oxide

lupeol

4. The bisdiazo compound $N_2CH(CH_2)_2CHN_2$ and cyclopentanone react to form a ketone (**1**), $C_9H_{14}O$ which in turn reacts with pertrifluoroacetic acid to give (**2**), $C_9H_{14}O_2$. Alkaline hydrolysis of (**2**), followed by acidification of the reaction mixture permits the isolation of (**3**), $C_9H_{16}O_3$ which furnishes (**4**), $C_9H_{14}O_3$ on oxidation with acidic chromium trioxide. Wolff–Kishner reduction of (**4**) gives cyclooctanecarboxylic acid. Deduce the structures of compounds (**1**) to (**4**) and discuss the mechanism for the conversion of (**1**) into (**2**).

5. Discuss the mechanisms of the solvolytic rearrangements of the following brominated longifolene derivatives under identical conditions and

suggest why the replacement of a methyl group with a carbomethoxy group should alter the outcome of the reaction.

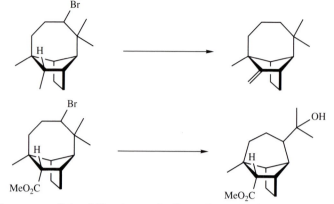

6.   Treatment of the following optically active α-hydroxyketal under the conditions shown led to the formation of a methyl ester with the same level of optical activity. Suggest a mechanism to rationalise this observation.

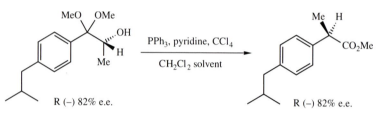

Further reading

For an account of the history of the elucidation of terpene rearrangements see J. Simonsen and L. N. Owen, *The Terpenes*, Cambridge University Press, Cambridge, 1949 Vol. II, and J. A. Berson, in *Molecular Rearrangements*, ed. P. deMayo, Wiley Interscience, New York, 1963, Part 1. Chapter 1 of this book, written by Y. Pocker, gives a useful overview of general aspects of Wagner–Meerwein shifts and pinacol rearrangements.

J. Mann, *Secondary Metabolism*, 2nd edn., Oxford Science Publications, Oxford, 1986, Chapter 3, gives a concise overview of terpene biogenesis and molecular rearrangements in these systems.

For   discussions of transannular hydride shifts see A. C. Cope, M. M. Martin, and M. A. McKervey, *Quart. Rev.(London)*, 1966, **20**, 119 and V. Prelog and J. G. Traynham, in *Molecular Rearrangements*, ed. P. deMayo, Wiley Interscience, New York, 1963, Part 1.

3. Nucleophilic rearrangements to carbon involving carbanions and carbenes

3.1 Introduction

The Wagner–Meerwein and related rearrangements considered in Chapter 2 are characterised by the requirement for a high degree of carbocationic character at the migration terminus in order to initiate rearrangement. While constituting a very important sub-division of nucleophilic rearrangements, not least for their historical significance, such carbocation induced shifts are by no means the whole story. Since the migrating terminus simply has to be electron deficient relative to the group undergoing migration, it is not necessary to involve full carbocations.

In many nucleophilic rearrangements it may be simply sufficient for the migration terminus to possess a leaving group, and in such cases the migrating species is frequently negatively charged. In comparing Wagner–Meerwein type rearrangements with such anion induced rearrangements it is useful to draw the analogy of nucleophilic substitution reactions, considering the former to be related to an internal S_N1 process and the latter to an internal S_N2 process. Synthetically useful anion induced processes include the Favorskii and Ramberg–Backlung rearrangements.

In another synthetically very important group of nucleophilic rearrangements, electron deficiency at the migration terminus is provided by generation of a valence satisfied but coordinatively unsaturated carbene.

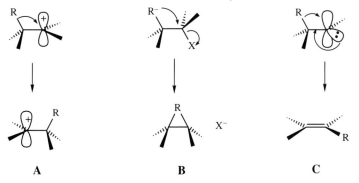

A   **B**   **C**

General mechanistic types of nucleophilic rearrangements to carbon termini:

A   carbocation induced;   B   carbanion initiated;   C   carbene induced.

A
singlet carbene

B
triplet carbene

The most frequently encountered carbene induced nucleophilic rearrangement, the Wolff rearrangement, generates the carbene centre by loss of nitrogen from α-diazoketone substrates and may be used to effect ring contraction of cyclic ketones or homologation of carboxylic acids, the latter procedure being known as the Arndt–Eistert synthesis.

A useful formalism to adopt when dealing with mechanisms involving carbenes is to consider the carbene centre to be 'C^{+} $^{-}$', as it is then much easier to see how to push curly arrows. In fact 'C^{+} $^{-}$' is a means of representing *singlet carbene* which possesses an empty *p*-orbital with the spin-paired non-bonding electrons residing in one sp^2-orbital. The alternative electronic configuration is *triplet carbene* in which the electrons reside in different atomic orbitals. Generally, dihalocarbenes have singlet ground states whereas carbene itself and alkyl carbenes have triplet ground states. The different electronic configurations of singlet and triplet carbenes result in differences of reactivity of these species in electrocyclic reactions but both undergo the same sorts of rearrangements.

3.2 Nucleophilic rearrangements intitiated by base

The Favorskii rearrangement

The Favorskii rearrangement refers to the skeletal reorganisation of α-halogenated carbonyl compounds on reaction with alkoxides to furnish esters.

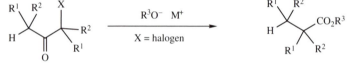

It is named after its discoverer who, in 1894, first reported the conversion of dichloroketones to unsaturated carboxylic acids on heating with potassium carbonate. However, the Favorskii rearrangement can be applied to a wide range of different α-halogenated ketones and finds a particularly useful application in the conversion of cyclic substrates to ring contracted carboxylic acid derivatives.

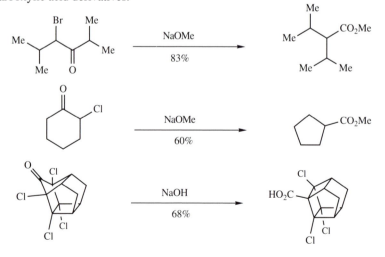

An interesting example of a double Favorskii ring contraction is the key step in the synthesis of the architecturally fascinating compound 'cubane'. In this reaction two fused α-bromocyclopentanone units were contracted to cubane dicarboxylic acid which was subsequently decarboxylated.

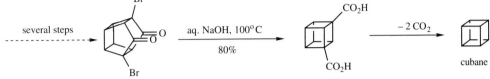

The actual mechanism of the rearrangement has been the subject of intense study and it is generally accepted that the conversion proceeds *via* a reactive cyclopropanone intermediate. The mechanism therefore occurs by initial deprotonation at the α'-position followed by intramolecular displacement of the halide to generate an intermediate cyclopropanone which is opened under the reaction conditions to furnish the carboxylic acid derivative (an ester, acid or amide depending upon the nucleophile used). The net effect of this process is the nucleophilic migration of an alkyl group from the carbonyl carbon to the α-position with loss of halide.

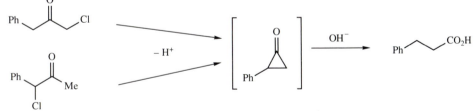

Very strong evidence for this cyclopropanone mechanism is provided by the observation that certain isomeric substrates form the same ester. A consequence of such a mechanism is that the structure of the initial chloroketone should have little influence upon the outcome of the reaction, the structure of the product ester resulting from the direction of ring opening of the cyclopropanone intermediate. This has been found to be the case.

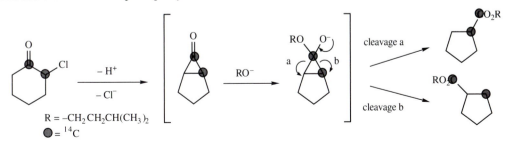

Compelling evidence for the intermediacy of cyclopropanone species comes from the observation that 2,3-double ^{14}C labelled 2-chlorocyclohexanone gives cyclopentane carboxylic acid with one label remaining on the carbonyl carbon and the other label split equally between C-1 and C-2.

The observation that both C-1 and C-2 were labelled to the same extent is in keeping with the equal likelihood of cleavage at either of the two bonds to the carbonyl group of the cyclopropanone intermediate. Further evidence to support this mechanism is provided by the observation that cyclopropanones prepared by other means react with alkoxides to give the predicted ester products, although cyclopropanone intermediates have not been isolated from the Favorskii reactions.

The exact timing of the cyclopropanone formation step has also been the subject of much scrutiny. It is generally accepted that there is a discrete initial deprotonation, with carbanion formation preceding loss of halide, as loss of stereochemical information is usually observed at the migration origin, in keeping with the formation of a planar enolate. Stereochemical evidence has indicated that, in certain circumstances at least, attack by the carbanion occurs simultaneously with loss of halide in an S_N2 type ring closure. For instance, the diastereomeric substrates in the following scheme led selectively to diastereomeric acid rearrangement products with no stereochemical crossover occurring. The relationship between the product and starting material in each case shows that an inversion of configuration has occurred at the chlorine bearing terminus.

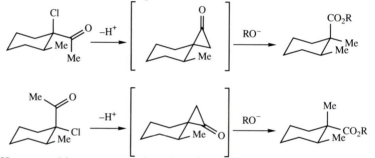

However, this stereocontrol at the migration terminus is not observed in solvents such as methanol, and this may be due to an S_N1 type of process occurring in the polar medium, in which a dipolar intermediate is formed.

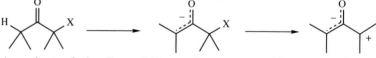

A variant of the Favorskii reaction occurs with α,α- and α,α'-dihaloketones which lead to the production of α,β-unsaturated esters. The reaction has also been carried out on α,β-epoxyketones which give β-hydroxycarboxylic acid derivatives.

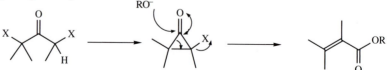

A further variant, sometimes referred to as the *quasi Favorskii rearrangement* is demonstrated by α-halocyclobutanones and α-haloketones which do not possess a hydrogen at the α'-position. Substrates of this nature cannot rearrange *via* cyclopropanone intermediates and instead undergo a base catalysed pinacol type rearrangement, sometimes referred to as a *semibenzilic rearrangement*.

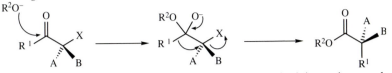

This proposed mechanism, implies a stereochemical inversion at the migration terminus and this has been demonstrated experimentally using the conformationally locked α-bromocyclohexyl phenyl ketone shown below.

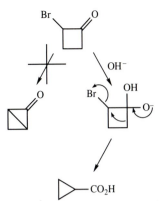

Quasi Favorskii rearrangement of α-bromocyclobutane.

A few examples of Favorskii rearrangements in substrates other than α-haloketones have been reported. For instance, certain α,β-epoxyketones afford hydroxy acids and the corresponding lactones on treatment with base, and a procedure has been developed in which α-hydroxyketones may undergo a similar conversion on treatment with diethyl carbonate and sodium hydride. In this latter reaction, use of carbonyl oxygen ^{18}O labelled substrate confirmed the intermediacy of a cyclopropanone.

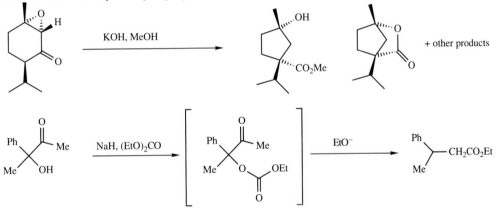

The Ramberg–Bäcklund rearrangement

This is another rearrangement which involves the formation of a cyclic intermediate and refers to the base promoted conversion of α-halosulphones into alkenes with the extrusion of sulphur dioxide. These substrates do not readily undergo substitution of the halogen by external nucleophiles. Instead exposure to base results in deprotonation at the α'-position, the protons of which are relatively acidic due to stabilisation of the resultant anion by the adjacent sulphone group. Generally α-halosulphones possessing an α'-hydrogen readily undergo the reaction to give mixtures of alkene geometric isomers, the ease of reaction increasing in the order Cl ≪ Br < I. The cyclic intermediate is called an *episulphone* or *thiirane dioxide* and these compounds, prepared by other routes, are known to eliminate sulphur dioxide readily upon heating by a process known as *cheletropic extrusion*.

Protons α- to a sulphone group are relatively acidic due to resonance stabilisation of the resultant anion.

A *cheletropic* reaction is defined as one in which two σ- bonds terminating at a single atom are made or broken in a concerted manner.

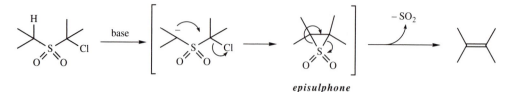

episulphone

This rearrangement is particularly useful for preparing alkenes in small rings or highly substituted alkenes as the alkene is not formed until the final very favourable extrusion step.

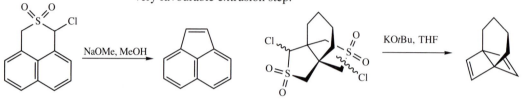

The benzil–benzilic acid rearrangement

This rearrangement is named after the parent reaction but is not restricted solely to aromatic α-diketones as aliphatic diketones and α-ketoaldehydes will also undergo the reaction.

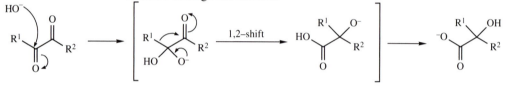

The process is irreversible and use of an alkoxide in place of hydroxide leads directly to the corresponding ester. However, a side reaction is possible with readily oxidised alkoxide groups such as Me_2CHO^- (these reduce the starting material to the corresponding α-ketol), and phenoxides are insufficiently basic to participate in the reaction. A similar reaction may be initiated by carbon nucleophiles.

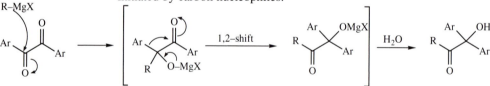

3.3 Nucleophilic rearrangement involving carbenes

The Wolff rearrangement

Aliphatic diazo compounds are generally far too labile to isolate under normal conditions. However, the presence of a carbonyl group renders these substrates much more stable and α-diazoketones are readily prepared by the nucleophilic attack of diazoalkanes on acid chlorides with subsequent loss of chloride and deprotonation. Despite this enhanced stability compared to their simple aliphatic counterparts, α-diazoketones readily undergo decomposition to liberate the very stable nitrogen molecule and a neutral, valence unsatisfied carbene. This tendency to decompose rapidly, liberating a gaseous product makes α-diazoketones liable to explode and they need to be handled with great caution and their isolation is avoided wherever possible. The decompositon can be carried out either thermally or by photolysis and, depending upon the reaction conditions, the carbene may be formed in either the singlet or the triplet state (see page 36). Whilst the nature of the carbene has fundamental effects upon its reactivity in reactions such as cycloadditions, it is irrelevant to the outcome of the Wolff rearrangement in which a 1,2-nucleophilic migration of the alkyl residue attached to the carbonyl group occurs to form a ketene intermediate. There has been much debate about the timing of the mechanism and many attempts to distinguish between the two step process involving the intermediacy of a carbene or a concerted process in which migration occurs at the same time as loss of nitrogen.

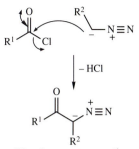

α–Diazoketone preparation.

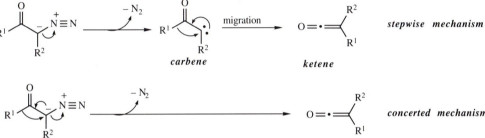

stepwise mechanism

concerted mechanism

The general concensus appears to be that carbenes are intermediates in the photochemically initiated Wolff rearrangement but there is still controversy about the thermal process. The situation is further complicated by the fact that the carbene intermediate appears to exist in equilibrium with a cyclic isomer called an **oxirene**. The existence of this equilibrium has been demonstrated by the equal distribution of ^{14}C label in the acid produced by the photochemically induced rearrangement of carbonyl labelled 2-diazobutan-3-one in the presence of water. A carbene intermediate would have given an acid which only possessed labelling at the carbonyl carbon.

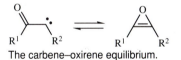

The carbene–oxirene equilibrium.

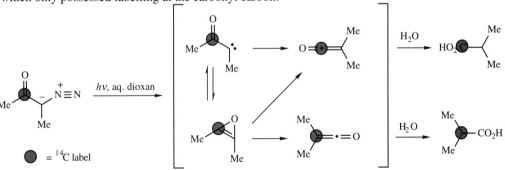

Studies on the thermal reaction have indicated that there is no observable kinetic isotope effect if the migrating carbon is ^{14}C which favours a stepwise process in which the rate determining step is the generation of the carbene. Generally the thermal reaction is carried out in the presence of silver salts which catalyse the decomposition of the diazoketone. Invariably the reaction is carried out in the presence of water, alcohols or aqueous ammonia when the product is the carboxylic acid, ester or amide resulting from attack of solvent on the ketene intermediate produced by the migration step. The overall conversion is directly equivalent to that achieved by Favorskii rearrangement of α-haloketones (see pages 36–39).

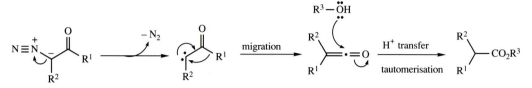

Wolff rearrangements are of particular utility in preparing ring contracted carboxylic acids *via* cyclic α-diazoketones.

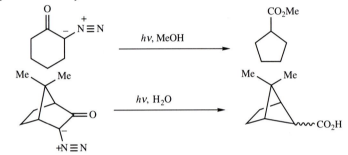

The Wolff rerrangement finds a neat industrial application in certain lithographic plates known as *diazo plates*. In essence a lithographic plate consists of a metal sheet coated with a thin layer of polymer to which is bound a photosensitive material. Selective irradiation of areas of the plate through a mask representing the image to be captured results in photochemical reaction in the exposed areas. This alters the properties of the irradiated coating, either hardening it (*negative working*) or rendering it soluble (*positive working*). In diazo plates the photosensitive material is one of a family of *ortho*-napthoquinone diazides. These undergo Wolff rearrangement on irradiation to produce carboxylic acids by reaction with traces of water present in the film.

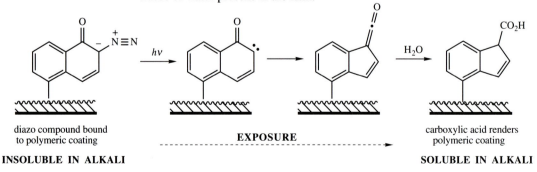

The principle behind photochemical development of diazo lithographic plates.

This sequence renders the exposed areas soluble in aqueous alkali and they can be stripped from the plate, leaving behind the unexposed areas of coating which can then be used to transfer ink to another surface — usually paper. Colour pictures may then be constructed by superimposing images from a series of four different plates, each corresponding to a different primary colour or black.

The Arndt–Eistert homologation

As α-diazoketones are most conveniently prepared from the reaction of diazoalkanes with acid chlorides, themselves derived from carboxylic acids, Wolff rearrangement in the presence of water results in a sequence by which a carboxylic acid may be converted to its homologue. This procedure is of such importance that it is usually referred to as the *Arndt–Eistert homologation.*

$$R-CO_2H \xrightarrow{SOCl_2} R-COCl \xrightarrow{CH_2N_2} R-\overset{-}{C}O\overset{+}{C}HN_2 \xrightarrow[\text{heat}]{AgO, H_2O} RCH_2-CO_2H$$

In order to minimise side reactions leading to the formation of α-haloketones of the type $RCOCH_2Cl$, it is usual to add the acid chloride to an excess of diazomethane. It is neither necessary, nor desirable to isolate the intermediate diazoketone. The overall yields for the three step sequence are usually in the region of 50–80%. Examples of the application of the Arndt–Eistert homologation in synthesis include the preparation of norprogesterone and the conversion of α-amino acid derivatives to their β-amino acid analogues such as the γ-glutamyl peptide shown below.

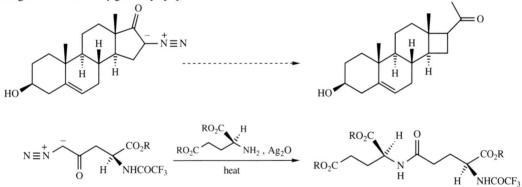

3.4 Exercises

1. Rationalise the following sequence, and identify intermediates:

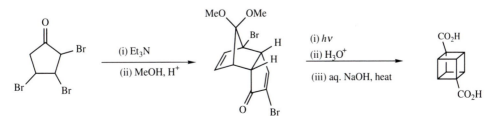

2. Identify the products from the following reactions:

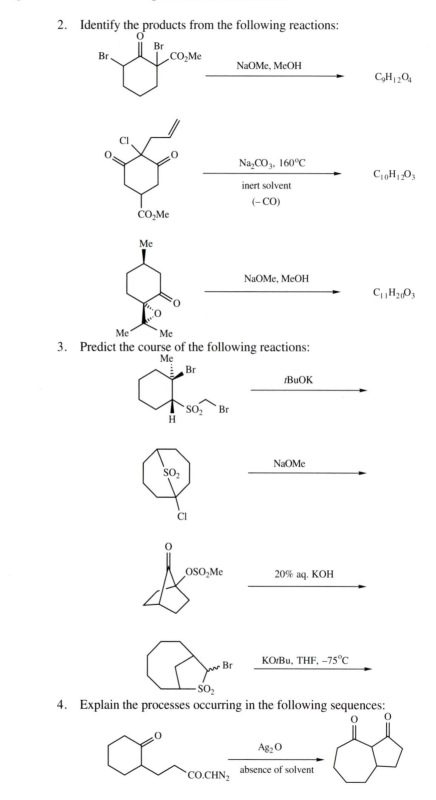

3. Predict the course of the following reactions:

4. Explain the processes occurring in the following sequences:

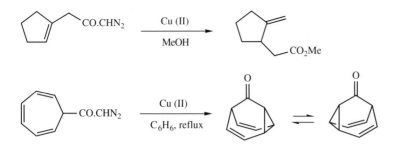

Further reading

For a review of the Favorskii reaction see: A. S. Kende, *Org. React.*, 1960, **11**, 261.

For reviews of the Ramberg Backlund reaction see F. G. Bordwell, in *Organosulfur Chemistry*, ed. M. J. Janssen, Interscience, New York, 1967, Chapter 16; L. A. Paquette, *Acc. Chem. Res.*, 1968, **1**, 209; *Org. React.*, 1977, **25**, 1.

For reviews of the Wolff and Arndt Eistert reactions see: W. E. Bachmann and W. S. Struve, *Org. Reactions*, 1942, **1**, 38 (Arndt Eistert synthesis); H. Meier and K.–P. Zeller, *Angew. Chem., Int. Edn. Engl.*, 1975, **14**, 32.

4. Rearrangements to electron deficient nitrogen and oxygen

4.1 Introduction

This far we have only discussed nucleophilic 1,2-alkyl shifts to carbon termini, but now we will turn our attention to two very important classes of rearrangement in which the migration terminus is either an electron deficient nitrogen or oxygen atom.

In the case of nucleophilic rearrangements to nitrogen, migration could be considered to occur concurrently with displacement of a substituent from the nitrogen, or by a stepwise process involving initial fragmentation to form a *nitrene* at the terminus, followed by migration.

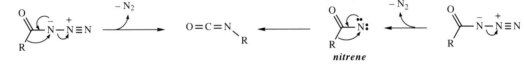

concerted migration　　　　　　　　　　　　　　　*stepwise migration involving a nitrene*

nitrene　　　*carbene*

Nitrenes and carbenes are *isoelectronic*. Both are neutral species which have a sextet of electrons in their outer shell.

Nitrenes are neutral, six electron species analogous to carbenes and react in a similar manner with nucleophilic species to regain an octet of valence electrons. While nitrenes are implicated in certain transformations, there is little support for their intermediacy in the migration reactions we will be considering in this chapter and the rearrangements are generally considered to follow concerted mechanisms with migration occurring at the same time as loss of the leaving group. In these reactions, it is the departure of a leaving group from the nitrogen which initiates rearrangement and may also control which group migrates. This contrasts with nucleophilic 1,2-migrations to carbon when factors such as relative migratory aptitudes of the migrating groups control the course of reaction.

Nucleophilic rearrangements to electron deficient oxygen involve peroxy species and are initiated by protonation and heterolytic cleavage of the labile peroxide bond. As with electron deficient nitrogen induced rearrangements, the migration usually occurs in concert with the breaking of the peroxy-linkage.

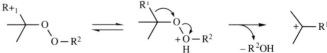

Both types of rearrangement have great synthetic utility and a reflection of this is the confusing number of named reactions which follow the same general mechanism. We shall now consider these various examples, but always bear in mind that they are all closely related and follow the same fundamental mechanism just outlined.

4.2 Rearrangements to electron deficient nitrogen

The Beckmann rearrangement

Treatment of oximes with reagents which convert the hydroxyl into a leaving group results in rearrangement to form a secondary amide. Often phosphorus pentachloride is used to initiate migration but concentrated sulphuric acid, polyphosphoric acid, formic acid, thionyl chloride, and silica have all been applied with success in specific cases. Commonly the group which migrates is the one *anti-* to the hydroxyl group and this is taken to indicate a high degree of concertedness in the rearrangement , with the alkyl group migration occurring in a synchronous manner with loss of the leaving group to generate a ***nitrilium ion***. Note that this is in complete contrast to the pinacol rearrangement discussed in Chapter 2 where the nature of the rearrangement depends upon the relative migratory aptitudes of the migrating species

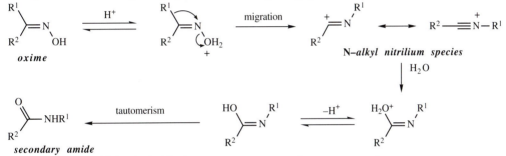

However, stereospecificity in the Beckmann rearrangement is not as general as may be implied in some texts. Sometimes the group which was *syn-* to the hydroxyl is found to have migrated and, even more commonly, mixtures of amides may be formed — particularly if R^1 and R^2 are both alkyl groups. This does not invalidate the mechanism shown above as oximes are known to undergo ready *syn–anti* isomerism under the types of acidic condition used to initiate rearrangement but it does require caution in adopting over-simplistic explanations.

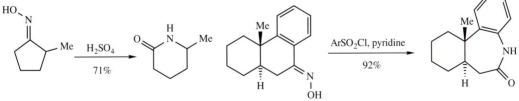

Examples of stereospecific Beckmann rearrangements.

Oximes derived from aldehydes are not usually good substrates for Beckmann rearrangement and yields of primary amides obtained in this manner are commonly poor. However, cyclic ketones undergo a very useful

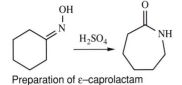

Preparation of ε–caprolactam

ring enlargement to give cyclic lactams and this reaction forms the basis of the industrial production of ε-caprolactam, an important feedstock chemical for the preparation of nylon 6 by alkaline polymerisation. In the laboratory cyclic ketones can be converted to lactams in a 'one-pot' process using hydroxylamine sulphonic acid in the presence of formic acid *via* sequential conversion to the oxime sulphonate and Beckmann rearrangment.

With certain substrates, particularly those in which one of the substituents on the oxime is a tertiary alkyl group or possesses a β-heteroatom substituent, a nitrile may be formed by a fragmentation process instead of a rearrangement. This '*second order Beckmann reaction*' is a consequence of the enhanced stability of the carbocation produced under these circumstances.

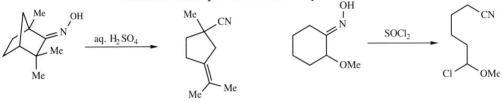

Another variant involves the reaction of toluenesulphonate derivatives of oximes with organoaluminium reagents when the intermediate nitrilium ion is attacked by the organometallic nucleophile. In this manner, oximes may be converted to imines.

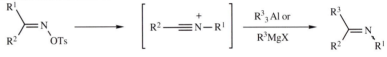

The Neber rearrangement

Ketoxime toluenesulphonates may also be rearranged in the presence of base, when Beckmann type side reactions are suppressed, to yield α-aminoketones; although aldoximes do not undergo this reaction. The mechanism involves initial deprotonation at the migration origin (for this reason the reaction is more efficient if this group is benzylic) and internal displacement of the leaving group to form an intermediate *azirine*. Subsequent attack by water on work-up gives the product.

azirine

Unlike the Beckmann rearrangement, the Neber rearrangement shows no dependence upon the stereochemistry of the oxime sulphonate. Instead it is the substituent possessing the most acidic α-position which migrates. There is some debate as to whether deprotonation and internal displacement of the arylsulphonate group are stepwise as shown in the diagram, or concerted. Similarly it has been suggested that the formation of the azirine might proceed by stepwise loss of the toluenesulphonate group from the deprotonated intermediate to form a nitrene before cyclisation to the azirine.

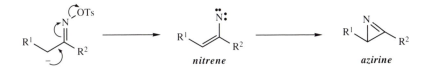

The Curtius rearrangement

This reaction, and the Lossen and Schmidt rearrangements considered next, provides the means for degrading a carboxylic acid to a primary amine containing one less carbon atom and all bear a generic similarity. In the Curtius rearrangement the key step is the thermal conversion of an acyl azide to an isocyanate. The acyl azides are usually prepared by the action of sodium azide on an acid chloride or by the action of nitrous acid upon hydrazides. Azides must be treated with caution as they may decompose explosively.

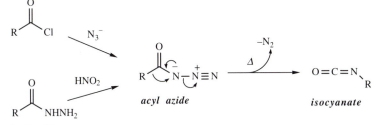

The sequence is very useful for preparing isocyanates as it may be carried out under non-aqueous conditions; nevertheless, the usual course of events involves subsequent hydrolysis of the isocyanate. If the solvent is an alcohol the product is the corresponding carbamate ester, but if the solvent is water the initial adduct undergoes subsequent decomposition to liberate carbon dioxide and an amine.

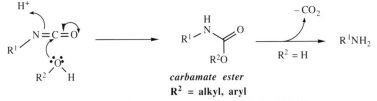

The rearrangement step has some analogies with the Wolff rearrangement (see pages 40–43) although the Wolff rearrangement proceeds *via* a carbene intermediate whereas the Curtius rearrangement is almost certainly concerted and does not involve the intermediacy of a nitrene. However, there is evidence to support the existence of nitrene species when *tertiary alkyl* azides undergo Curtius rearrangement to form imines.

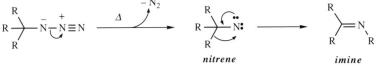

This reaction may also be carried out at lower temperatures using an acid catalyst, although these conditions usually result in hydrolysis of the imine to the corresponding ketone.

The Lossen rearrangement

The Lossen rearrangement refers to the conversion of *O*-acylhydroxamic acids to isocyanates on treatment with base and is mechanistically very similar to the Curtius rearrangement. As the reaction is normally carried out in water, the process furnishes the amine directly. However, the relative difficulty in obtaining hydroxamic acids which are used to prepare the rearrangement precursors means that this method is used less frequently than the Curtius or Schmidt rearrangements.

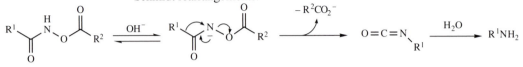

The Schmidt reaction

The commonest version of the Schmidt reaction involves the acid catalysed addition of hydrazoic acid to a carboxylic acid to furnish initially a protonated acyl azide. This subsequently undergoes rearrangement to form an isocyanate which is then hydrolysed with decarboxylation to form an amine. Effectively the rearrangement step is the same as in the Curtius rearrangement and it is only in the means of generation of the acyl azide that these sequences differ. The reaction works well for aliphatic carboxylic acids but less so for aromatic carboxylic acids. However, sterically hindered aromatic substrates such as 2,4,6-trimethylbenzoic acid (mesitoic acid) give good yields and this provides support for the view that the initial step is an example of the rare $A_{AC}1$ type of process for ester cleavage which occurs under strongly acidic conditions (concentrated sulphuric acid is commonly used). Thus, protonation of the hydroxylic oxygen followed by loss of water leads to the formation of an *acylium* ion which is then attacked by the hydrazoic acid to form the protonated acyl azide which undergoes rearrangement. The rearrangement and subsequent steps are the same as in the Curtius rearrangement.

$A_{AC}1$ = First order acid catalysed acyl cleavage.

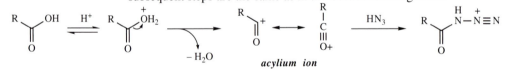

acylium ion

However, unlike the Curtius and Lossen rearrangements, carbonyl compounds, alcohols, and alkenes can also be substrates. In fact dialkyl ketones react more readily than carboxylic acids. In the case of ketones, the end product is the amide in which the nitrogen has been inserted between the carbonyl carbon and the substitutent. Once again the reaction requires strongly acidic conditions, and diaryl ketones are sufficiently unreactive that chemoselectivity between diaryl and dialkyl ketones is possible.

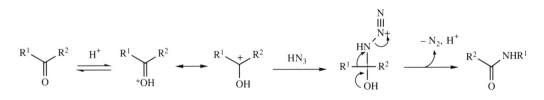

There is little control over which group migrates; although with aryl alkyl ketones it is usually the aromatic group which does so. Aldehydes, which are not such good substrates for this reaction, give rise to nitriles although further hydrolysis under the reaction conditions is possible. Nitrile formation may also be a troublesome side-reaction with ketones, particularly those in which a substituent may be lost as a stable carbocation.

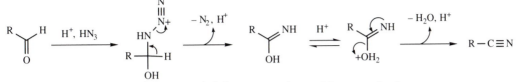

Cyclic ketones yield ring expanded lactams and provide a synthetic alternative to the Beckmann rearrangement.

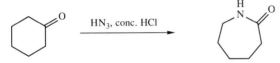

Alcohols and alkenes react to form alkyl azides which, under the reaction conditions undergo further rearrangement to form imines with subsequent hydrolysis as discussed in the sub-section covering the Curtius reaction.

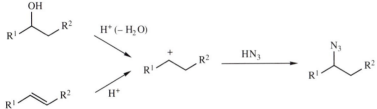

The Hofmann rearrangement

Primary amides, on treatment with aqueous sodium hypobromite (usually generated *in situ* from bromine and sodium hydroxide), undergo a degradative rearrangement to give an amine containing one carbon atom less than the starting amide. This procedure can be particularly useful for degrading aromatic amides to amines. By now it should come as no surprise to learn that the mechanism involves the formation of an isocyanate by migration of the amide substituent from the carbonyl carbon to the nitrogen, followed by hydrolysis to the amine. However, the process by which the isocyanate is formed differs from those discussed previously.

The first step in the reaction sequence is the formation of the *N*-bromoamide which then undergoes removal of the remaining proton on the nitrogen, the acidity of which is enhanced due to the presence of the electronegative bromine in addition to the acyl group. The deprotonated intermediate subsequently undergoes rearrangement by what is generally accepted to be a concerted mechanism although a two step process involving loss of bromide and formation of a nitrene would also be compatible with the data available.

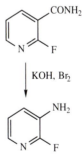

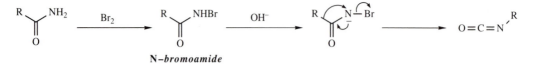

N–bromoamide

In a modification used for high molecular weight amides, methanol may be substituted for aqueous sodium hydroxide to form the methyl carbamate which may be isolated or hydrolysed as peviously described. Yields are low when aqueous sodium hydroxide is used with these substrates, presumably due to their low solubility in the reaction medium.

N–Alkyl ureas give hydrazines *via* an analogous reaction.

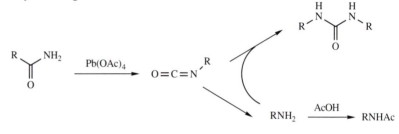

A similar type of conversion can be achieved by reacting primary amides with lead tetraacetate which converts the amide to the isocyanate and then to the amine, liberating acetic acid in the process. The amine can then react either with the acetic acid to form an ethanamide derivative or with the isocyanate to give a disubstituted urea.

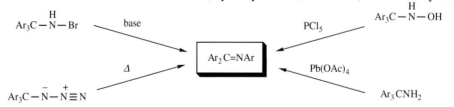

The Stieglitz rearrangement

This and a number of related rearrangements form a second, less commonly encountered class of reactions which fall into the category of nucleophilic migration from carbon to nitrogen. The Steiglitz rearrangement strictly refers to the rearrangements of various triarylmethylamines and trityl derivatives, such as *N*-haloamines, hydroxylamines, and azides, to form *N*-arylimines.

Trityl = Ph₃C–

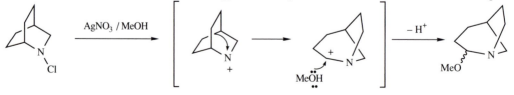

Certain cyclic *N*-chloroamines undergo solvolysis induced 1,2-migration on treatment with silver nitrate in polar solvents in a rearrangement which shows some analogy to the Wagner–Meerwein shifts discussed in Chapter 2.

A related example in which *N*-chloraminocyclopropanols are coverted into β-lactams on solvolysis has a mechanistic similarity with the pinacol rearrangement.

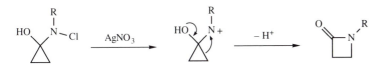

4.3 Rearrangements to electron deficient oxygen

The Baeyer–Villiger rearrangement

This is by far the most important reaction involving 1,2-migrations to an electron deficient oxygen terminus and has great synthetic utility as it permits the conversion of ketones into esters, while cyclic ketones generate lactones. Even more importantly the conversion often shows high regioselectivity with unsymmetrical substrates, the oxygen atom being 'inserted' between the carbonyl carbon and the most substituted α-carbon. The relative ease of migration increases in the order Me < RCH_2 < Ar < R_2CH < R_3C. The methyl group has such low migratory aptitude in the Baeyer–Villiger rearrangement that oxygen insertion between a carbonyl and a methyl group never occurs in practice. With aromatic groups, electron donating groups increase the migratory aptitude and electron withdrawing groups decrease it. Aldehydes also react, usually by migration of the hydrogen to give carboxylic acids.

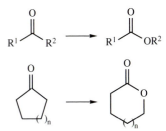

Conversions possible with the Baeyer–Villiger rearrangement.

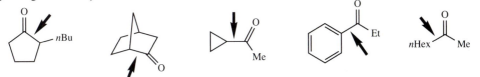

Sites of oxidation of some representative ketones.

The reaction is conveniently accomplished by oxidation with peracids, and peracetic acid, 3-chloroperbenzoic acid and magnesium monoperoxyphthalate are all convenient to use. For more reluctant substrates such as ketones with primary alkyl residues, trifluoroperacetic acid is the reagent of choice, although its strong acidity usually requires the reaction mixture to be buffered. For example, cyclohexanone reacts 200 times more rapidly with trifluoroperacetic acid than with peracetic acid. Other reagents which have been used to accomplish the same conversion include H_2O_2–$BF_3.Et_2O$ and $K_2S_2O_8$–H_2SO_4. One limitation of this reaction is that double bonds present in the molecule are frequently epoxidised and thioethers oxidised to sulphoxides or sulphones.

The reasons for the regioselectivity of the reaction and the enhanced reactivity of trifluoroperacetic acid can be explained by consideration of the reaction mechanism. The first step involves nucleophilic attack of the peracid at the carbonyl carbon of the protonated ketone to give a tetrahedral intermediate, often referred to as the *Criegee intermediate* after the proposer of the mechanism. This then collapses to regenerate the sp2-centre by 1,2-nucleophilic migration of one of the alkyl substituents to the adjacent oxygen with concomitant loss of the carboxylic acid. The overall reaction pathway shows similarities to carbonyl homologation with diazomethane.

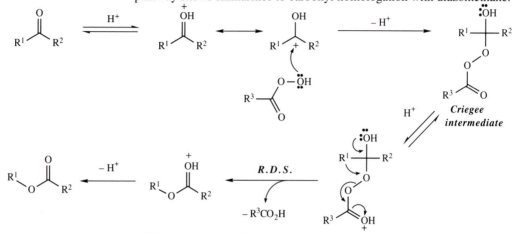

Note that in the above mechanistic scheme the rearrangement has been shown to occur on the protonated Criegee intermediate. Indeed, the Baeyer–Villiger reaction is catalysed by acid, but it also proceeds in the absence of strong acids and so another rearrangement pathway, operating through the unprotonated Criegee intermediate with loss of carboxylate anion, must also be possible.

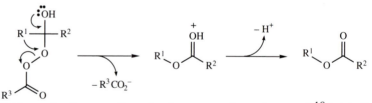

Evidence for the overall mechanism comes from the use of ^{18}O labelled acetophenone, when the oxygen label in the product ester is found to reside totally in the carbonyl oxygen. Observation of a kinetic isotope effect using C-1 ^{14}C labelled aryl groups is interpreted to mean that the migration is involved in the rate determining step and therefore must occur in concert with loss of the carboxylic acid residue. In keeping with a concerted mechanism, chiral groups have been demonstrated to migrate with retention of absolute stereochemistry.

From consideration of the above mechanism it is possible to understand why trifluoroperacetic acid is the reagent of choice for Baeyer–Villiger reactions. The inductive electron withdrawing effect of the three fluorine atoms stabilises any negative charge on the carboxylate group. One immediate effect of this is that trifluroacetic acid ($pK_a = 0.2$) is a far stronger acid than acetic acid ($pK_a = 4.70$. Consequently, trifluoracetate is a better *nucleofuge* than acetate and therefore is more readily lost in the rearrangement step.

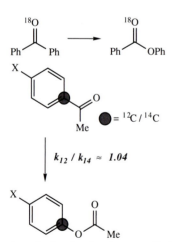

A *nucleofuge* is a leaving group that takes away an electron pair.

The relative migratory aptitude of different substituents in the Baeyer–Villiger reaction (Me < RCH$_2$ < Ar < R$_2$CH < R$_3$C) can be related to the ability of the group to sustain a positive charge in the transition state which in turn implies the involvement of some sort of bridged non-classical species in the migration step. It is often forgotten that the nature of the peracid can have a modifying effect upon the reaction, with the more reactive trifluoroperacetic acid lowering the selectivity, but the underlying migratory aptitudes still expressing themselves. For instance, phenyl cyclohexyl ketone rearranges 90% *via* cyclohexyl migration with peracetic acid, but with trifluoroperacetic acid the proportion drops to 80%.

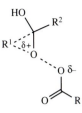

The Baeyer–Villiger reaction achieves an extremely useful synthetic conversion and this, together with its ease, selectivity, and generality has made it a popular choice of chemists involved in total synthesis. One example which illustrates the power of the reaction is the preparation of a key intermediate for the total synthesis of a wide range of physiologically active molecules called prostaglandins. The intermediate is now usually known by the name of 'Corey lactone', after the 1990 Nobel Prize winning chemist E. J. Corey who introduced it. Many variants of its synthesis have been developed but all utilise a Baeyer–Villiger oxidation to convert a norbornenone to a lactone, setting up three centres of relative stereochemistry. Note that the regioselectivity of the oxidation is in keeping with that predicted on the basis of substitution at the α-position to the carbonyl group. In this instance chemoselective conversion of the ketone to a lactone is possible in the presence of an alkene. For steric reasons norbornenes selectively undergo epoxidation from the *exo*-face, but in this instance this face is sterically protected by the pendant benzyl ether moiety.

exo– attack favoured

endo– attack disfavoured

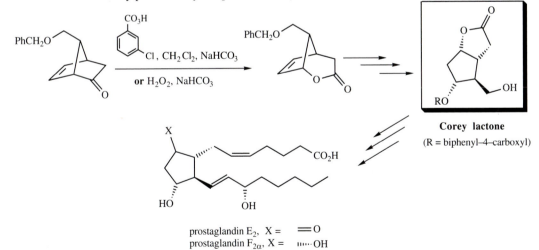

Corey lactone
(R = biphenyl–4–carboxyl)

prostaglandin E$_2$, X = ═O
prostaglandin F$_{2\alpha}$, X = ⅲ⋯OH

The hydroperoxide rearrangement

Treatment of hydroperoxides with Brönsted or Lewis acids results in cleavage of the peroxide bond and concomitant 1,2-migration of a neighbouring substituent. The relative migratory aptitude of groups is R$_3$C > R$_2$CH >

alkyl groups. Migration gives rise to an intermediate which is hydrated to form a *hemiacetal* which readily hydrolyses to a carbonyl compound and an alcohol under the acidic aqueous conditions. The carbocationic intermediate formed by the migration has been observed spectroscopically in super-acid media at low temprature.

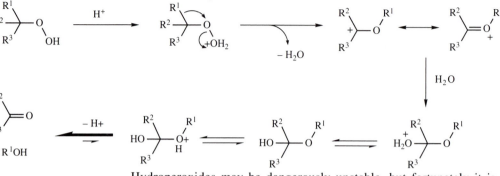

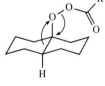

Hydroperoxides may be dangerously unstable, but fortunately it is not necessary to isolate them as treatment of alcohols with hydrogen peroxide in the presence of acids will promote the whole process. Treatment of primary alcohols in this way provides a means of conversion to lower homologues.

Ether and ester derivatives of hydroperoxides also undergo similar rearrangements. Indeed, the earliest rearrangement involving hydroperoxides was observed in 1904 and involved a hydroperoxide ether. In this example bis(triphenylmethyl) hydroperoxide was found to form triphenylmethyl chloride and dichlorodiphenylmethane on heating with phosphorus pentachloride, but it was not for a further 27 years that the equivalent rearrangement of triphenylmethyl hydroperoxide was reported. Criegee reported the first hydroperoxide ester rearrangement in 1944 in which the acetate and benzoate esters of 9-hydroperoxy-*trans*-decalin were found to rearrange spontaneously, giving 6-hydroxycyclodecanone after hydrolysis.

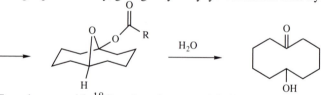

Experiments with ^{18}O carbonyl oxygen labelled substrates gave a product ketol containing no label. This has been rationalised by invoking formation of a '*tight ion pair*' on migration, with the carboxylate residue rebonding through the same oxygen. If the carboxylate residue had become a free entity, the two oxygens would be chemically indistinguishable and roughly half of the label would be incorporated into the ketol.

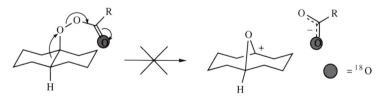

Tert-butyl acetate and benzoate have been shown to undergo rearrangement *via* initial *homolytic* O–O bond cleavage, but the corresponding trifluoroacetate rearranges by an ionic process. Diacyl peroxides show such great susceptibility to undergo homolytic cleavage into two carboxyl radicals that this dominates their chemistry. However, catalysis of the decomposition by acid suggests that heterolytic decomposition can play some role.

The Dakin reaction

Aromatic aldehydes and ketones possessing a hydroxyl or amino group in either the *ortho-* or *para*-position can be converted to phenols on treatment with alkaline hydrogen peroxide. The conversion occurs *via* hydrolysis of the corresponding esters which are formed by a rearrangement process bearing a strong mechanistic resemblance to the Baeyer–Villiger reaction. The carbonyl carbon is attacked by the hydroperoxide anion and the tetrahedral intermediate then collapses with migration of the aryl group from carbon to the neighbouring oxygen with displacement of hydroxide. The ester thus formed undergoes hydrolysis under the aqueous alkaline conditons of the reaction; although ester intermediates have been isolated, lending support to the proposed mechanistic rationale.

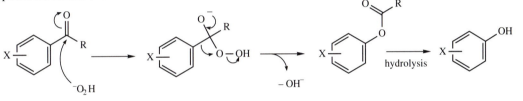

X = *o–* or *p–* OH or NH$_2$

Electron releasing substituents are necessary for efficient migration of the aromatic group, the electronic requirement having a direct analogy with the Baeyer–Villiger reaction. With benzaldehyde, hydride migration is favoured over the phenyl group to give benzoic acid almost exclusively.

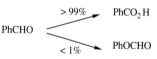

4.4 Exercises

1. Give mechanisms to account for the formation of the following products under the reaction conditions specified.

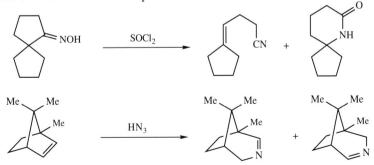

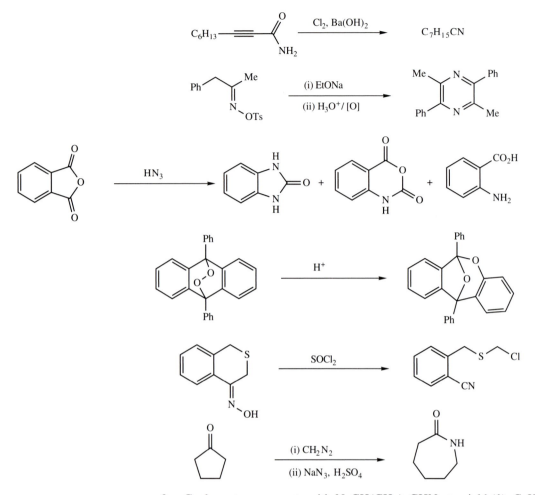

2.   Cyclopentanone reacts with $N_2CH(CH_2)_2CHN_2$ to yield (**1**), $C_9H_{14}O$ which reacts with trifluoroperacetic acid to give (**2**), $C_9H_{14}O_2$. Alkaline hydrolysis of (**2**) gives (**3**), $C_9H_{16}O_3$, which on sequential oxidation with CrO_3 in acetic acid and Wolff–Kishner reduction yields cyclooctane carboxylic acid. Identify (**1**), (**2**), and (**3**) giving your reasoning.

3.   Suggest possible reasons for the following observations:

(a) Baeyer–Villiger oxidation of camphor with Caro's acid (H_2SO_5) yields the unexpected rearrangement product in 30% yield; whereas norcamphor yields the expected product.

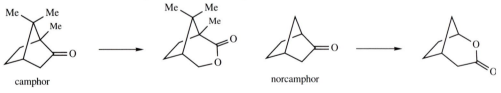

camphor   norcamphor

(b) The rate of Baeyer–Villiger oxidation of 4-substituted cyclohexanones increases in the order H < Me < tBu.

Further reading

For a discussion of whether or not nitrenes are involved in migrations to electron deficient nitrogen see: W. Lwowski, *Nitrenes*, Interscience, New York, 1970, pp. 217–21.

For reviews of the Beckmann rearrangement see: C. G. McCarty, *The Chemistry of the Carbon–Nitrogen Double Bond*, ed. S. Patai, Wiley Interscience, New York, 1970, pp 408–39; L. G. Donaruma and W. Z. Heldt, *Org. React.*, 1960, **11**, 1.

The Neber rearrangement has been discussed by C. O'Brien, *Chem. Rev.*, 1964, **64**, 81.

For surveys of the Curtius, Lossen, Schmidt, and Hofmann reactions as processes for converting carboxylic acids to amines possessing one less carbon atom see: E. S. Wallis and J. F. Lane, *Org. React.*, 1946, **3**, 267 (Hofmann); H. Wolff, *Org. React.*, 1946, 3, 307 (Schmidt); P. A. S. Smith, *Org. React.*, 1946, **3**, 337 (Curtius). In this last chapter the relative merits of the reactions are compared.

The Baeyer–Villiger rearrangement has been extensively reviewed. For instance see: H. O. House, *Modern Synthetic Reactions*, 2nd edn., Benjamin, New York, 1972, pp. 321–9; J. B. Lee and B. C. Uff, *Quart. Rev.*, 1967, **21**, 429.

Aspects of the Dakin reaction are discussed by W. M. Schubert and R. R. Kintner, *The Chemistry of the Carbonyl Group*, ed. S. Patai, Interscience, New York, 1966, Vol 1, pp. 749–52.

5. Electrophilic rearrangements

5.1 Introduction

With the exception of *prototropic* rearrangements (H^+ migrations), electrophilic rearrangements — in other words those rearrangements in which a group migrates formally as a cationic species — are far less commonly encountered than the nucleophilic types of rearrangement we have considered up to now. This is largely due to the fact that an intramolecular electrophilic rearrangement, has four electrons involved in the transition state one pair of which has to be accommodated in an antibonding orbital of the migrating species.

The situation can be visualised most easily by considering the migration to be an intramolecular S_N2 reaction and looking at the frontier molecular orbitals of the migrating group and the migration terminus. In the initial species, the anionic migration terminus acts as the nucleophile and hence we must consider the *highest occupied molecular orbital* (HOMO) at this centre interacting with the *lowest unoccupied molecular orbital* (LUMO) of the migrating group. In the initial anionic species the non-bonding *p*-orbital on the migration terminus is the HOMO. During the initial stages of migration, the pair of electrons in this orbital begins to interact with the LUMO of the the migrating group which is the *antibonding* σ-orbital. As the reaction proceeds to completion, the original bonding electrons finish in the non-bonding orbital at the migration origin and the remaining pair form a σ-bond between the migrating group and migration terminus. This is a grossly over-simplified picture, but serves our purpose at this level.

1,2-electrophilic rearrangements can be considered as intramolecular S_N2 reactions.

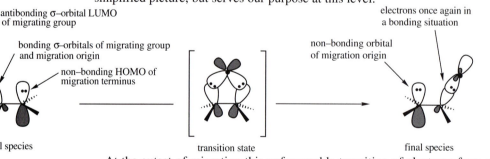

antibonding σ-orbital LUMO of migrating group

bonding σ-orbitals of migrating group and migration origin

non-bonding HOMO of migration terminus

electrons once again in a bonding situation

non-bonding orbital of migration origin

initial species   transition state   final species

At the outset of migration this unfavourable transition of electrons from a non-bonding into an antibonding orbital means that the reaction possesses a high activation energy barrier and is kinetically disfavoured. Note that, with our hypothetical symmetrical system, there is no overall energy change but, in practice, unsymmetrical substrates lead to electrophilic rearrangements in which the product is more stable than the starting material. The process then becomes thermodynamically favourable, although kinetically disfavoured.

In addition to molecular orbital considerations, the positioning of the antibonding orbital on the migrating group requires rear-side attack of the migration terminus upon the migration centre, and places additional steric constraints upon electrophilic migrations.

As a consequence of the above reactivity requirements, the migrating group is usually an aromatic ring which is better able to accommodate the additional pair of electrons. As we shall see shortly, the constraints of a concerted migration are so strong that, when electrophilic rearrangements do occur, that they probably do so in a stepwise manner and not *via* a concerted mechanism.

In all of the examples we will consider, rearrangement is initiated by generation of a carbanion at the migration terminus. The most commonly encountered and synthetically useful electrophilic rearrangements involve migration of a group from a heteroatom (nitrogen, sulphur, or oxygen), but some rearrangements with a carbon atom at the migration origin are known.

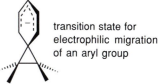

transition state for electrophilic migration of an aryl group

5.2 Rearrangements from nitrogen

The Stevens rearrangement

If a quaternary ammonium salt possessing an electron withdrawing group α- to the nitrogen is treated with base an *ylid* can be generated which may rearrange in such a manner that the overall result is transfer of one of the remaining nitrogen substituents to the deprotonated position. The reaction is named after T. S. Stevens, who was responsible for discovery of this rearrangement in 1928 and carried out investigations into its mechanism.

Crossover experiments showed the mechanism to be intramolecular and migration of groups with an asymmetric α-position led to products in which the stereochemical information at that centre had been retained. These data were originally considered to rule out an elimination–addition process which would involve loss of stereochemical integrity of the migrating centre. Instead they were interpreted to indicate a pathway proceeding by α-deprotonation followed by concerted electrophilic migration with inversion of the absolute stereochemistry of the migrating group. The stereochemical inversion would give the required stereochemistry for a concerted migration proceeding by an intramolecular S_N2 mechanism.

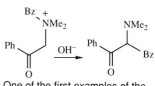
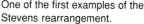

One of the first examples of the Stevens rearrangement.

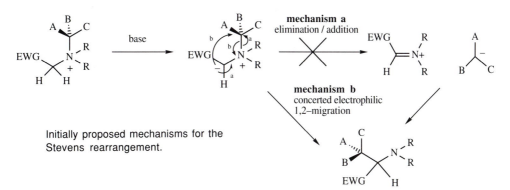

Initially proposed mechanisms for the Stevens rearrangement.

However, further studies demonstrated that rearrangement occurs with *retention* of absolute stereochemistry at the migrating centre and later spectroscopic examination indicated that free radical intermediates are formed during the reaction. Subsequently this has led to the adoption of the mechanism, shown in the following diagram, involving deprotonation followed by homolytic cleavage to generate a pair of radicals. In such a mechanism it is necessary to invoke a rapid recombination of the radicals which do not escape from a tight solvent cage in order to explain the observed intramolecularity and the lack of racemisation. In fact it is now thought possible that some reactions may involve the addition–elimination process (originally discarded on the basis of lack of racemisation) with the ion pairs remaining trapped in a solvent cage.

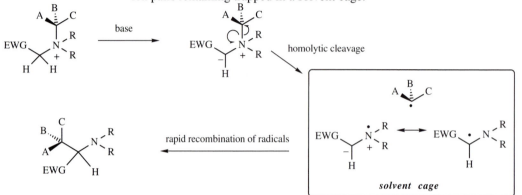

Addition of more than one equivalent of base results in little increase in reaction rate and this is interpreted as meaning that complete anion formation precedes any rearrangement. Substrates often possess a carbonyl group β- to the quaternary nitrogen and this serves to ease anion formation further. When the migrating group is benzylic, electron withdrawing substituents on the aromatic nucleus increase the rate of rearrangement.

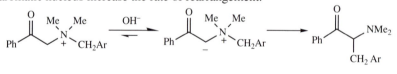

Ar	4-methoxyphenyl	4-methylphenyl	4-chlorophenyl	4-nitrophenyl
Relative rate	0.76	1.06	2.65	73.0

A variant of this reaction occurs with sulphonium salts which are deprotonated, forming a sulphur ylid which subsequently rearranges in a directly analogous manner to the more usually encountered nitrogen based Stevens rearrangement. Once again there is spectroscopic evidence pointing to the intermediacy of tightly bound radical pairs. Elimination of the resultant thioether provides a synthetic alternative to the Ramberg–Bäcklund reaction.

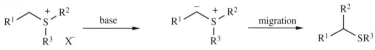

sulphonium salt   *sulphur ylid*

The Sommelet–Hauser rearrangement

This rearrangement is related to the Stevens rearrangement often competing with it, and may even supercede it. The reaction bears the name of its French discoverer M. Sommelet who, in 1937, reported that trimethyl (diphenylmethyl)ammonium hydroxide rearranged on standing to give (2-benzyl)benzyldimethylamine. Similar by-products are obtained when Stevens rearrangements are carried out on benzyl trialkylammonium substrates. The reaction became synthetically useful with the discovery in 1951 by C. R. Hauser that the use of alkali metal amides in liquid ammonia led to almost total exclusion of Stevens type rearrangement products. The reaction mechanism involves initial deprotonation of the benzylic position which is in equilibrium with a second ylid. It is this ylid which, despite being present as the minor species, undergoes 2,3-sigmatropic rearrangement to generate the product after reprotonation. The lack of crossover with labelled substrates is taken as strong evidence that rearrangement does not occur by a dissociation–recombination process, although the small amount of material resulting from migration to the *para*-position may be formed by such a mechanism. Whilst polar sigmatropic rearrangements are largely dealt with in chapter 7, the Sommelet–Hauser rearrangement is covered here due to its close relationship with the Stevens rearrangement.

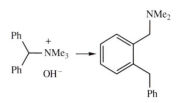

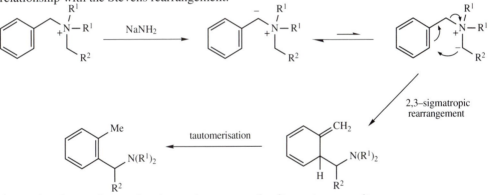

As the product is a tertiary amine, it may be converted to its quaternary salt and the process repeated if there is a free *ortho*-position available.

The Meisenheimer rearrangement

Once again this reaction bears a close resemblance to the two preceding reactions. In this case a tertiary *N*-oxide undergoes thermal rearrangement to furnish the corresponding *O*-substituted hydroxylamine.

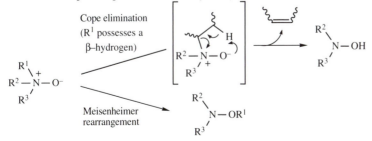

The migrating group is usually benzylic or allylic and the remaining groups may be alkyl or aryl. However, if any of the groups possesses a β-hydrogen, Cope elimination predominates, limiting the synthetic utility of this rearrangement.

5.3 Rearrangements from oxygen

The Wittig rearrangement

The Wittig rearrangement is directly analogous to the Stevens rearrangement in mechanism and outcome (not be confused with the better known *Wittig reaction*) and takes its name from Georg Wittig who carried out definitive investigations into the mechanism of the reaction after its discovery in 1924 by Schörigen. Compared with the Stevens rearrangement stronger bases, such as *n*-butyllithium or sodium amide, are used to initiate Wittig rearrangement as the reaction proceeds *via* negatively charged species, rather than ylid formation as is the case in the nitrogen series. There is no restriction upon the nature of the oxygen substituents as long as there is at least one hydrogen present α- to the oxygen; although many functionalities will not be able to withstand the strongly basic conditions. As with the Stevens rearrangement, a radical pair mechanism is probably operating with each of the pair of radicals recombining before escaping from the solvent cage. Migratory aptitudes are in the order allyl ≈ benzyl > alkyl > methyl > aryl, with electron withdrawing substituents increasing aryl group migratory aptitude.

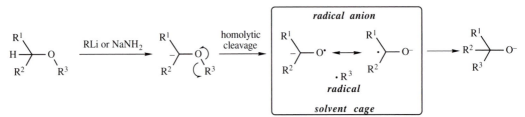

The evidence for such a mechanism is strong. Crossover experiments have demonstrated that the rearrangement is largely intramolecular, although some leakage can occur, consistent with a tightly bound dissociative pathway. The migratory aptitudes are in accord with relative radical stability and chiral groups have been found to migrate with partial racemisation; although the main pathway results in retention of configuration. The same type of product also results if ketyl radicals and alkyl radicals prepared from different starting materials are combined.

When R^3 is allylic a concerted 2,3-sigmatropic rearrangement can operate.

In all cases the driving force for reaction is the conversion of the initial carbanion to the thermodynamically more stable alkoxide.

5.4 Rearrangements from sulphur

We have already seen that a variant of the Stevens rearrangement involves generation of a sulphur ylid and its subsequent rearrangement. The following pair of reactions are most commonly encountered with sulphur as the migration origin.

The Smiles and Truce–Smiles rearrangements

The Smiles rearrangement refers to an intramolecular nucleophilic aromatic substitution and the general mechanism can be shown as follows:

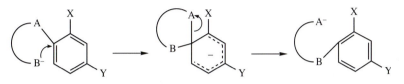

X and / or Y = electron withdrawing group

Both A and B are heteroatoms in the Smiles rearrangement. Commonly the heteroatom A is S, SO, or SO_2 (although examples are also known where A is O), and B may be O, NR, or S. In the Truce–Smiles modification, B is a carbon centre and in this latter case, it is not necessary for electron withdrawing groups to be present on the migrating aryl group.

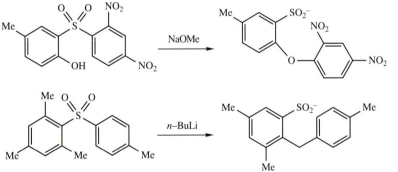

Smiles rearrangement

Truce–Smiles rearrangement

Although the couple of examples shown above possess two aromatic rings, the chain linking A–B can also be aliphatic. In cases where this second ring is aromatic however, an important accelerative effect is noted for those substrates possessing an additional substituent at C-6. The basis for this effect can be shown to be steric rather than electronic as isomeric substrates with the substitutent at C-4 rearrange about 10^5 times more slowly.

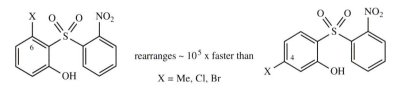

rearranges ~ 10^5 x faster than

X = Me, Cl, Br

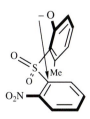

This effect is due to the fact that the favoured ground state conformation for the 2,6-buttressed substrate is close to that required for migration.

5.5 Carbon to carbon electrophilic migration

The exceptional ease with which many substrates undergo *carbocation* induced 1,2-migration of alkyl groups compares starkly with the dearth of examples in which the equivalent *carbanion* induced rearrangement occurs. Indeed, only in very exceptional circumstances, when steric and electronic effects combine, are such rearrangements found to occur.

This type of rearrangement is however found to occur in metallation reactions of 1,1,1-triaryl-2-haloalkanes, when it is not possible to detect the initial carbanion, the rearranged species being the sole detectable material present.

$$Ph_3CCH_2Cl \xrightarrow{2\ Na} Ph_2\bar{C}CH_2Ph\ \ Na^+$$

Clearly the driving force for this reaction is the relief of steric compression from C-1 and the greater stabilisation of the rearranged carbanion compared with the initially formed primary anion.

As the process of metallation of halides occurs *via* two single electron transfers, it is possible to envisage that rearrangement actually occurs after formation of the intermediate radical species before the second electron has been transferred.

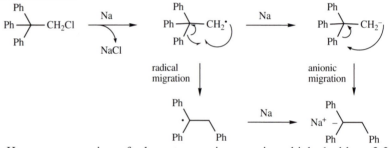

However, a series of elegant experiments, in which 1-chloro-2,2-diphenylpropane was metallated followed by a CO_2 quench have demonstrated that anion formation very probably precedes migration. The study found that 2,2-diphenylpropyl magnesium chloride was stable at temperatures up to 100°C with carbonation yielding 3,3-diphenylbutanoic acid. The lithio-derivative however, was found to be stable at 0 °C but rearranged at 40 °C, and the potassium derivative yielded only the rearrangement product.

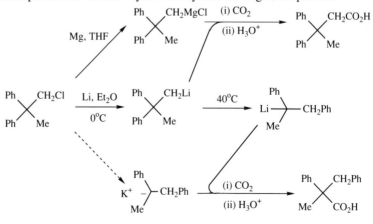

The progressive ease of rearrangement in the series Mg < Li < K was proposed to be a consequence of the increasingly ionic nature of the carbon–metal bond. Note that the alternative migration of the methyl group was not observed, despite the fact that this would have led to the more stabilised rearranged carbanion. This is in accord with the greater ability of the phenyl group to stabilise the negative charge during migration.

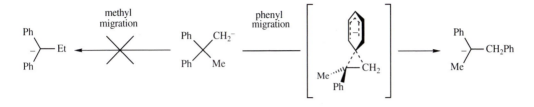

5.6 Exercises

1. Suggest mechanisms for the following reactions:

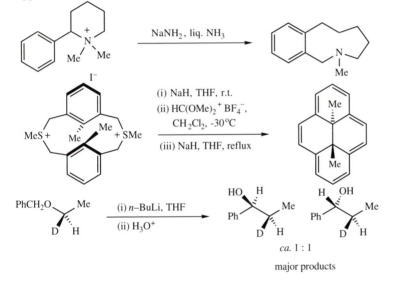

2. Explain the different pathways operating in the examples shown below:

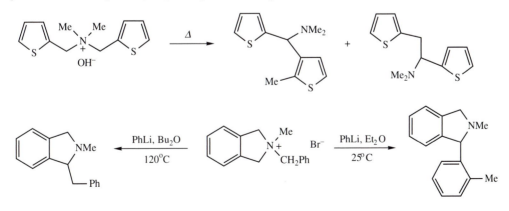

Further reading

For a really excellent introduction to the principles involved in the application of frontier molecular orbital theory to chemical reactivity consult I. Fleming, *Frontier Orbitals and Organic Chemical reactions*, Wiley, New York, 1977.

For reviews of the electrophilic rearrangements in general see H. E. Zimmerman, in *Molecular Rearrangements*, ed. P. de Mayo, Interscience, New York, 1963, Chapter 6.

For reviews relating to specific reactions see: S. H. Pine, *Org. React.*, 1970, **18**, 403 (Stevens and Sommelet–Hauser); R. K. Olsen and J. O. Currie, *The Chemistry of the Thiol Group*, ed. S. Patai, Wiley, New York, 1974, Vol. 2, pp. 561–6 (sulphur variant of the Stevens); R. A. W. Johnstone, *Mech. Mol. Migr.*, 1969, **2**, 249 (Meisenheimer); U. Schöllkopf, *Angew Chem., Int. Ed. Engl.*, 1970, **9**, 763 (Wittig rearrangement); W. E. Truce, E. M. Kreider, and W. W. Brand, *Org. React.*, 1971, **18**, 99 (Truce –Smiles).

6. Acid catalysed aromatic rearrangements

6.1 Introduction

In this chapter we must plunge yet again into the realm of arbitrary distinction in order to create this classification of 'aromatic rearrangements'. Many of the reactions we will consider here are initiated by the generation of an *arenium ion* and involve migration either around the aromatic ring, or from a side chain onto the aromatic nucleus. In all cases the migration terminus is a position on an aromatic ring. Such reactions are initiated either by protonation or by a Lewis acid and are commonly a consequence of equilibration to form the thermodynamically most stable products.

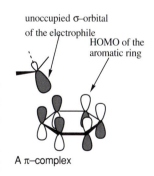

arenium ion

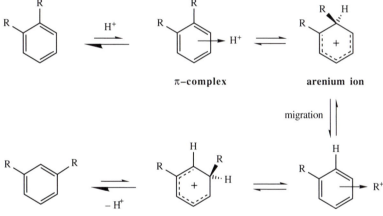

General mechanism of the acid catalysed rearrangement of aromatic substrates

Intramolecular migration is believed to occur *via* a π-complex which leads to equilibration between arenium ion species. The notation for π-complexes, as shown in the above reaction sequence, indicates that the electrophilic species is coordinated to the entire π-system and is positioned above the plane of the aromatic ring. The orbital interactions involve the lowest unoccupied orbital of the electrophilic partner (LUMO) and the highest occupied molecular orbital (HOMO) of the aromatic ring (benzene has two degenerate HOMOs). It is this extended *p*-system that provides the means for migration. In the case of alkyl group migration over the ring, the LUMO is a σ-orbital and, as a result, asymmetric alkyl groups migrate with retention of tetrahedral geometry and hence their absolute stereochemistry.

An intramolecular mechanism of rearrangement as outlined above is certainly attractive, but it is difficult to rule out a dissociation–reassociation process with certainty. The usual means of differentiation involves crossover experiments, but need not lead to valid results with aromatic rearrangements as the reactivities of the intermediate π-complexes and arenium ions are such as to permit additional intermolecular scrambling, despite the fact that the initiating reaction may be intramolecular.

Perhaps not surprisingly, the mechanism of arenium ion generation bears a close resemblance to the mechanism for electrophilic aromatic substitution, the two pathways differing in the way in which the initially generated arenium ion reacts. In electrophilic substitution H⁺ is lost to regenerate the aromatic ring; whereas in the rearrangement the group migrates to generate a new arenium ion. Indeed, aromatic migrations may be considered formally to be intramolecular electrophilic aromatic substitution processes. Perhaps the best illustration of this relationship is to consider the Fries rearrangement, which is effectively the intramolecular variant of the Friedel–Crafts acylation. In both cases an acylium ion undergoes substitution into an aromatic substrate with the important difference that the acylium ion precursor in the Fries rearrangement is the aryl ester substrate itself.

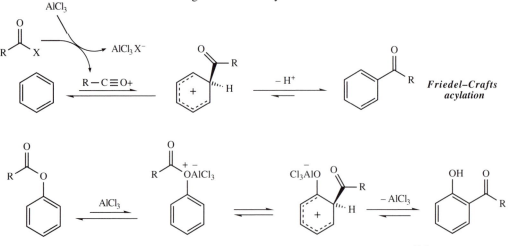

Friedel–Crafts acylation

Fries rearrangement

6.2 Acid catalysed rearrangements around the aromatic ring

Lewis acid catalysed equilibration of polyalkylbenzenes

Friedel–Crafts alkylation of aromatic compounds is rarely a synthetically useful reacton, usually resulting in complex mixtures of polyalkylated materials as the initial alkylation products are more electron rich and hence more reactive than the starting materials. Nevertheless, in studies it was noted that Friedel–Crafts alkylations carried out under non-forcing conditions (mild catalysts, low temperatures) gave rise to so-called 'normal' products in which the alkyl substituents bore 1,2- and 1,4-relationships to each other, in keeping with the known *ortho / para*- directing effect of alkyl groups.

In contrast to this, it was found that use of higher temperatures and longer reaction periods gave rise to increasing quantities of 1,3- and 1,3,5-

substituted materials. This changeover can be attributed to the equilibration of the initially formed products to form the thermodynamically most favoured products. For instance, heating 1,2-, 1,3- or 1,4-dimethylbenzene with catalytic quantities of HF–BF$_3$ resulted in the formation of the same equilibrium mixture, in agreement with the proportions expected from a consideration of the relative stabilities of the three isomers

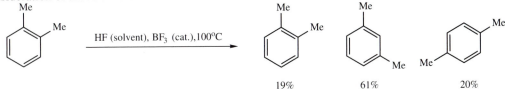

The equilibration is set up by initial complexation of the Lewis acid, followed by methyl group migraton in the resultant complex with subsequent liberation of the Lewis acid to continue the reaction cycle.

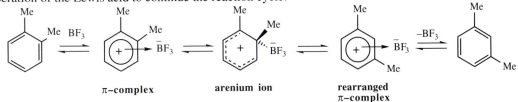

However, this is not the complete story as it was also found that use of higher concentrations of catalyst led to product mixtures in which the proportion of 1,3-dimethylbenzene approached 100%.

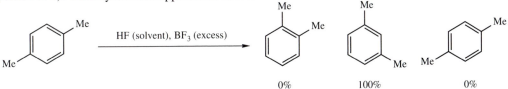

This effect is attributed to the fact that 1,3-dimethylbenzene is able to form stable complexes with the Lewis acid and is removed from the equilibrium. Disproportionation to toluene and trimethylbenzenes was found not to compete under the reaction conditions indicating that the intramolecular rearrangement is energetically more favourable than dissociation–reassociation pathways. The same effect was also noticed with HBr–AlBr$_3$ as the catalyst system and with HF–BF$_3$ on trimethyl and tetramethylbenzenes.

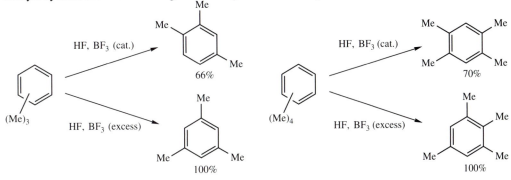

The Jacobsen rearrangement

A complementary rearrangement to the Friedel–Crafts related reactions just considered occurs when polyalkylated and polyhalogenated benzenes are heated with concentrated sulphuric acid to give the sulphonic acid derivatives in which rearrangement of the substituents has occurred. As the sulphonic acid group may be removed by heating with aqueous acid, the overall process results in reorganisation of the original substrate.

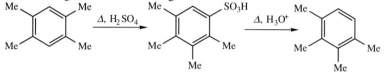

Although Herzig was the first to record the rearrangement of polyhalogenated benzenesulphonic acids in 1881, the mechanism is named after Oscar Jacobsen who described the reaction for polyalkylated benzenesuphonic acids in 1886. The brutality of the reaction conditions confines the application of the rearrangement to substrates possessing simple alkyl and halogen substituents and at least tetrasubstitution is necessary. However, within this limited substrate range, the Jacobsen rearrangement provides useful complementarity to the regiochemistry observed with Lewis acid promoted rearrangements. Whereas Lewis acids favour isomerisation to form 1,3-disubstituted and 1,3,5-trisubstituted systems, use of sulphuric acid results selectively in the formation of products in which the substituents have moved closer together leading to *vicinal* substitution.

The term *vicinal* is derived from the Latin *vicinalis*: neighbour.

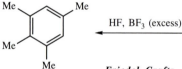

Friedel–Crafts   *Jacobsen*

The term *ipso* is derived from the Latin for *itself* and refers to the fact that substitution occurs at a carbon already possessing a substituent.

The reason for this complementarity becomes clear from a consideration of the probable reaction mechanism which involves *ipso*-sulphonation followed by intramolecular migration. This is believed to occur by a series of 1,2-nucleophilic shifts of the migrating group to give a rearranged arenium ion in which the sulphonate group is not destabilising the positive charge by resonance interactions.

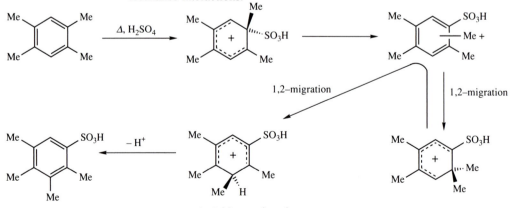

most stable arenium ion

A particularly ready rearrangement of octahydroanthracene-9-sulphonic acid occurs to give the isomeric octahydrophenanthrene-9-sulphonic acid.

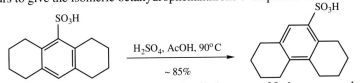

The dienone–phenol rearrangement detailed on page 28 shows a good deal of mechanistic analogy with the Jacobsen rearrangement.

Polyhalobenzenes do not undergo useful reaction on treatment with sulphuric acid, but halogenated polyalkylbenzenes often lead to rearrangement products in which the halogen has migrated selectively. For instance, 5-chloro- and 6-chloro-1,2,4-trimethylbenzenes are both converted to the same sulphonic acid by selective movement of the chlorine in each case.

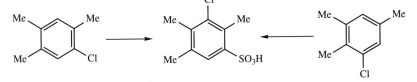

6.3 Acid catalysed rearrangements from side chains onto the aromatic ring

The Fries rearrangement

This reaction involves the Lewis acid catalysed conversion of aryl esters to acyl phenols. Rearrangement to either the 2- or the 4-position may occur and it is sometimes possible to select conditions to favour the formation of one isomer.

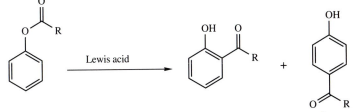

The ratio of products depends upon the temperature, solvent, and concentration of catalyst. It is usually the case that low reaction temperatures favour migration to the 4-position (*para*-Fries) and high temperatures favour migration to the 2-position (*ortho*-Fries).

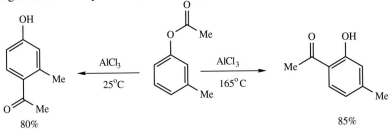

It should always be borne in mind that, despite the fact that the Lewis acid is a catalyst for the reaction, the acyl phenols produced by the rearrangement form complexes with the Lewis acid and so it is necessary to use more than one equivalent of reagent to ensure maximum conversion.

The acyl residue may be aromatic or aliphatic and esters possessing chains up to eighteen carbons long have been successfully rearranged. The relative rates of rearrangement of RCO have been shown to be in the order R = alkyl > benzyl > cinnamyl > phenyl. As the mechanism can be considered to be like an intramolecular electrophilic substitution process, electron withdrawing substitutents on the aromatic nucleus disfavour or totally block the reaction. For instance, rearrangement does not occur if the aromatic ring possesses a nitro-group at C-2 or C-4, or an acetyl group at C-4; while an acetyl group at C-2 severely inhibits it.

The mechanism of the Fries rearrangment has been much disputed, with contradictory evidence being produced to indicate that it is intermolecular *or* a dissociative intramolecular process *or* a true intramolecular migration.

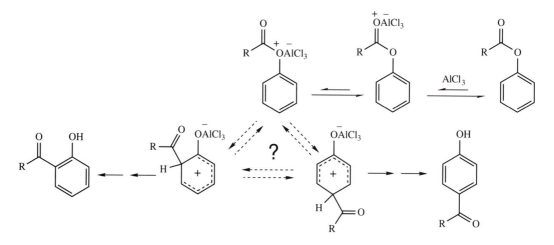

Certainly crossover experiments using two different ester substrates in the same reaction vessel have shown scrambling in some instances, but not in others. Nevertheless, bearing in mind the harshness of the reaction conditions, it is difficult to decide whether these results are meaningful or not. Other investigations have involved carrying out rearrangements in an aromatic solvent and looking for acylation of the solvent. However, once again it is not possible to interpret lack of solvent acylation as evidence for an intramolecular process as this result may simply be a consequence of the lower reactivity of the solvent. We are therefore left in the rather unsatisfactory situation of not knowing exactly how the actual rearrangement process occurs.

Some examples of a reverse Fries reaction have been found and this provides evidence to support the view that selective *ortho*-Fries rearrangement at high temperatures is a consequence of equilibration *via* the ester to form the thermodynamically most stable 4-acylphenol. Indeed, 4-acylphenols may be converted to 2-acylphenols on heating with aluminium chloride, although the intermediate ester has never been detected under these conditions.

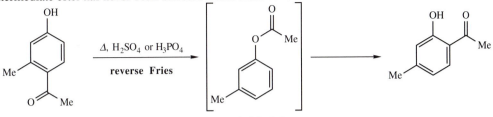

not detected

Although falling outside the area being covered in this book, it should be mentioned that a photochemical variant of the Fries rearrangement is known which has been shown spectroscopically to proceed *via* radical intermediates, the majority of which recombine before escaping their solvent cage.

Aryl ether rearrangement

By analogy with the Fries rearrangement, this reaction can be considered to be an intramolecular variant of the Friedel–Crafts alkylation, and it therefore should come as no surprise to learn that this isomerisation is synthetically much less useful than the Fries rearrangement.

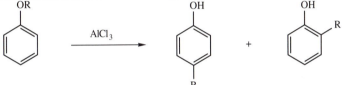

Dialkylphenols are common by-products from the reaction and, where possible, structural reorganisation of the alkyl side chain *via* 1,2-hydride migration occurs. The observation of dialkylphenols has been interpreted as indicative of a certain degree of intermolecularity but, conversely, the retention of some absolute stereochemistry during the migration of optically active alkyl groups provides evidence for intramolecular processes.

The *Claisen rearrangement* of allyl aryl ethers is normally carried out at elevated temperatures and proceeds *via* a concerted 3,3-sigmatropic rearrangement followed by tautomerisation of the resultant cyclohexadienone to regain the aromatic nucleus.

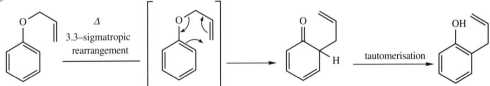

However, Brönsted and Lewis acids are known to catalyse this reaction, and under these conditions the rearrangement occurs after protonation or complexation of the substrate. This may involve a dissociative process, although, of course, a concerted sigmatropic rearrangement is still possible. The absence of crossover products or diallylated materials indicates that any dissociative process must involve tight ion pairs which recombine before diffusing away from each other.

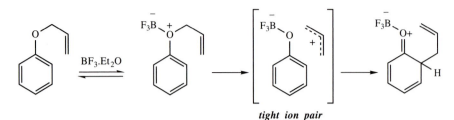

tight ion pair

Acceleration is dramatic under these conditions and Lewis acid catalysed rearrangements may occur at temperatures as low as –50°C.

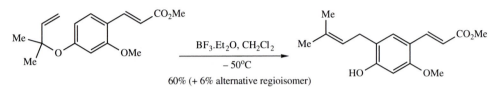

60% (+ 6% alternative regioisomer)

The Hofmann–Martius reaction

The corresponding rearrangement of alkylarylamines occurs on heating the hydrochloride salts to above 200°C.

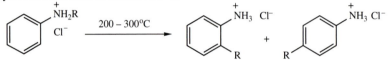

This rearrangement undoubtedly occurs by an intermolecular process, as polyalkylated products may be isolated from the reaction mixtures, and primary alkyl side chains are invariably isomerised, indicative of 1,2-hydride migration taking place in the initially formed primary carbocations (pp. 30–31). With primary alkyl groups, there is evidence that the mechanism involves formation of the alkyl halide, followed by Friedel–Crafts alkylation of the aromatic amine, as the ratio of 2- and 4-substitution products is dependent upon the halide counterion. A variant in which the alkylarylamine is heated with metal halides such as $ZnCl_2$ is sometimes referred to as the *Reilly–Hickinbottom rearrangement*, but this is restricted to primary alkyl groups as secondary and tertiary groups readily undergo eliminative cleavage.

Migrations of heteroatoms from nitrogen

Rearrangement of *N*-nitroarylamines on treatment with acid gives rise to the corresponding 2- and 4-nitro-derivatives.

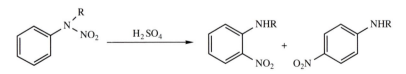

The migration is probably an intramolecular process, as rearrangements in the presence of $K^{15}NO_3$ show no incorporation of labelled nitrogen into the products. However, rearrangement of *N*-methyl-*N*-nitroaminobenzene gives appreciable quantities of *N*-methylaminobenzene and nitrous acid in addition to the expected 2- and 4-nitro-(*N*-methyl) aminobenzene and this points to a dissociative process leading to solvent caged species. This combined evidence indicates that homolytic cleavage of the protonated substrate occurs to form a radical and radical cation in tight association.

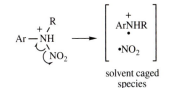

solvent caged species

Although at first sight very similar to the acid catalysed rearrangement of N–nitroarylamines, the corresponding reaction of N-nitrosoarylamines, known as the *Fischer–Hepp* rearrangement shows two important differences. Only HCl gives efficient rearrangement and, intriguingly, the 4-nitrosamines tend to be the exclusive products.

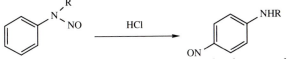

The preference for formation of 4–nitrosoarylamines would seem to indicate a dissociative process, but attempts to trap reactive intermediates such as nitrosyl chloride have been unsuccessful and so the mechanism of this rearrangement remains shrouded in mystery. Nevertheless, the reaction is synthetically useful as it provides one of the few means of access to 4-nitroso-(N-alkyl)aminobenzenes.

Aryl triazines also undergo acid catalysed rearrangement to form the corresponding 4-arylazo derivatives regioselectively; this time the reaction is probably intermolecular involving formation of ArN_2^+.

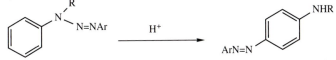

Treatment of arylhydroxylamines with acids leads to the formation of 4-aminophenols in an intermolecular process known as the *Bamberger rearrangement*.

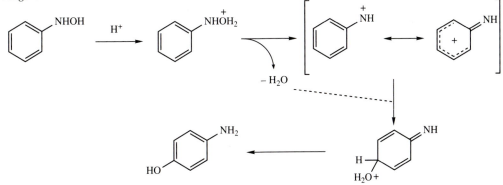

Evidence for the intermolecular nature of the reaction comes from competitive attack by other nucleophiles such as ethanol.

Isomerisation of N-halogenated N-arylamides to (4-haloaryl)amides on treatment with the corresponding acid HX is called the *Orton rearrangement*. It is commonly carried out on chloro- and bromo-amides.

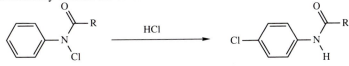

The fact that free halogen may be detected in the reaction mixture together with the evidence from crossover reactions has led to the proposal that the mechanism proceeds by reaction of HX with the haloamide to liberate the halogen and ArNHCOR. This then undergoes electrophilic substitution, predominantly at C-4 of the aromatic nucleus, possibly as a consequence of steric hindrance by the *N*-acyl group.

The Fischer indole synthesis

Treatment of arylhydrazones with Lewis or Brönsted acids (commonly $ZnCl_2$) results in formation of an indole with elimination of ammonia. It is not necessary to isolate the hydrazone and the reaction is very general as long as the starting carbonyl is of the form $R^1(CO)CH_2R^{2'}$.

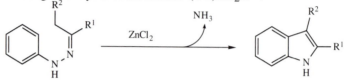

Hidden in this very useful method for constructing indoles is a polar rearrangement akin to the acid catalysed Claisen rearrangement, although nothing is known about the degree of concertedness or otherwise of this step.

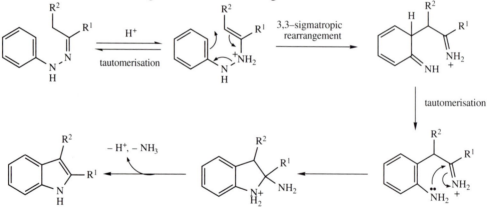

6.4 The benzidine rearrangement

Heating N,N′-diarylhydrazines (commonly referred to as hydrazobenzenes) with acids causes them to rearrange to form mixtures of 4,4′- and 2,4′-diaminobiaryls (**benzidines**, from which the rearrangement takes its name). The 4,4′-isomer usually predominates unless one or both of the 4- and 4′-positions of the diarylhydrazine are already substituted, although if these substituents are SO_3H, CO_2H or halogen the substituent may be displaced.

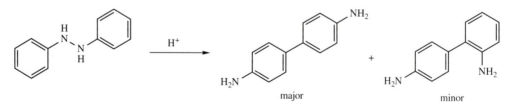

Other less commonly encountered side products of this reaction include the 2,2'-diaminobiaryl and 2'-and 4'-aminoarylanilines, the latter sometimes being referred to as *semidines*.

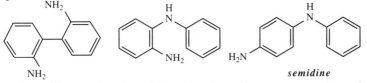

semidine

Another side reaction is *oxido-reductive disproportionation* of the diarylhydrazine to form $ArNH_2$ and $ArN=NAr$.

The reaction mechanism has been the subject of exhaustive investigation and several possibilities have been proposed, only to be discarded when new evidence came to light. The theory that a dissociative mechanism was operative could be ruled out by crossover experiments and the proposal that the semidines were intermediates in the reaction was conclusively discarded by the demonstration that the semidines cannot be converted into the diaminobiaryls under the reaction conditions.

A useful pointer to the mechanism came from kinetic studies. Whilst first order in hydrazine, the mechanism may be first or second order in H^+. Some substrates were found to be first order in H^+ at low acidity and second order at high acidity and to show fractional order at intermediate acidity. These data implicate the involvement of monoprotonated and diprotonated species in the rearrangement step. Conclusive information was obtained using isotopically labelled substrates to demonstrate that the two major diaminobiaryl products were the result of different pathways. With di-^{15}N-labelled substrate, the kinetic isotope effect for formation of the 4,4'-diaminobiaryl was 1.002; whereas for the 2,4'-diaminobiaryl it was 1.063. The observation of the kinetic isotope effects shows that cleavage of the N–N bond is involved in the rate determining step in each case, but the fact that they have different values proves that two different cleavage processes must be occurring. In addition, the use of 4,4'-di-^{14}C-labelled diphenylhydrazine gave an observable kinetic isotope effect of 1.028 for the formation of 4,4'-diaminobiphenyl indicating that C–C bond formation was also occurring in the rate determining step. These results can all be encompassed by the proposal that reaction occurs by means of a concerted 5,5-sigmatropic rearrangement of either the monoprotonated or diprotonated species.

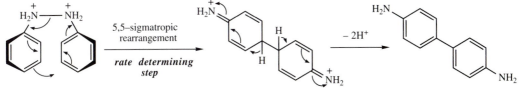

Although the scheme above shows the diprotonated species being formed prior to rearrangement, the second protonation step may take place during the rearrangement.

It is believed that C–C bond formation is not involved in the rate determining step for formation of the 2,4'-diaminobiaryl product but little more is known of the mechanism at this stage.

6.5 Exercises

1. Explain the following observations:

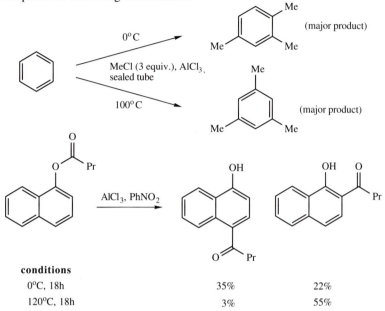

conditions		
0°C, 18h	35%	22%
120°C, 18h	3%	55%

2. Predict the major products on reaction of the following substrates under the conditions shown:

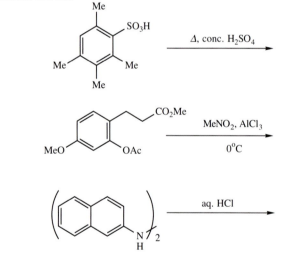

Further Reading

For reviews of aromatic rearrangements see: M. J. S. Dewar, *Molecular Rearrangements*, ed. P. de Mayo, 1963, Chapter 5; Vol. 1, Interscience, New York, D. L. H. Williams, *Comprehensive Chemical Kinetics*, ed. W. R. Bamford and C. F. H. Tipper, American Elsevier, New York, 1973, pp. 433–86; H. J. Shine, *Aromatic Rearrangements*, 1967.

For a discussion of the Jacobsen reaction see: L. I. Smith, *Org. React.*, 1942, **1**, 370.

The Fries rearrangement has been the subject of several reviews and monographs. For example see: A. H. Blatt, *Chem. Rev.*, 1940, **27**, 429 and *Org. React.*, 1942, **1**, 342; H. J. Shine, *Aromatic Rearrangements*, Elsevier, New York, 1967, pp. 72–82, 365-8, A. Gerecs, *Friedel–Crafts and Related Reactions*, ed. G. A. Olah, Interscience, New York, 1964, Vol. 3, pp. 499–533.

The Bamberger rearrangement has been reviewed by H. J. Shine, *Aromatic Rearrangements*, Elsevier, New York, 1967, pp. 182–190.

For a monograph on the Fischer indole synthesis see: G. M. Robinson, *The Fischer Indole Synthesis*, Wiley, New York, 1983.

The benzidine rearrangement has been reviewed by several authors. One such treatment is by R. A. Cox and E. Buncel, in *The Chemistry of the Hydrazo, Azo and Azoxy Groups*, pt. 2, ed. S. Patai, Wiley, New York, 1975, Part 2, pp. 775–807.

A thorough discussion of the '*π-complex mechanism*' of the benzidine rearrangement, together with a survey of other theories is presented by M. J. S. Dewar in *Molecular Rearrangements*, ed. P. de Mayo, Interscience, New York, 1963, Vol. 1, pp. 330–43.

7. Miscellaneous rearrangements

7.1 Introduction

Despite all attempts to classify polar rearrangements neatly into particular categories, based upon mechanistic or structural criteria, there are inevitably many reactions which fall outside any framework which might be devised. This final chapter is reserved for these reactions and the heading *'miscellaneous'* is simply a reflection of the diversity of the mechanisms. In this chapter we will consider some cationic processes in the section on allylic rearrangements, some sigmatropic migrations which rely upon total or partial charge separation, and a radical rearrangement in which the radical species are undoubtedly charged. It might be argued that some — or all — of these rearrangements should have been included in other chapters within this book, but none sits really comfortably into any of the previous categories, so they appear here.

7.2 Allylic rearrangements

Mechanisms

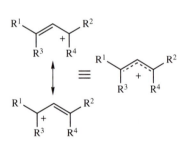

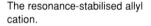

The resonance-stabilised allyl cation.

Allylic substrates are particularly prone to rearrange during nucleophilic substitution reactions. There are three major reaction pathways (S_N1', S_N2' and S_N1') by which rearrangement can occur, and these are directly analogous to the commonly encountered nucleophilic substitution mechanisms. Reaction under conditions which favour first order substitution (polar solvent, poor nucleophile, good leaving group) always leads to mixtures of isomeric products. This mechanism involves initial ionisation to form the resonance stabilised allylic cation. Under kinetic conditions, the site of nucleophilic attack is largely directed by the degree of positive character at each of the two carbons of the allylic resonance hybrid, with steric effects playing a secondary rôle. Consequently, it is impossible to avoid formation of mixtures of positional and geometric isomers in S_N1 reactions of acyclic allylic substrates under kinetic conditions.

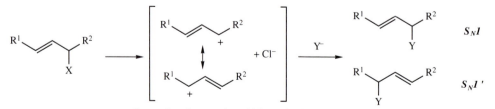

Second order nucleophilic substitution is favoured by reaction conditions involving strong nucleophiles, apolar solvents, and poor leaving groups.

With allylic substrates the S_N2' mechanism may compete with direct S_N2 reaction and the degree to which either occurs can sometimes be controlled. As a result, it may be possible to choose reaction conditions to obtain displacement with or without rearrangement.

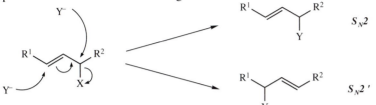

An additional feature of the S_N2' reaction is the possibility for the incoming nucleophile to approach from the same side as the leaving group, giving *syn*- attack, or from the opposite side in an *anti*- manner. The *syn*-pathway is usually predominant but the degree to which either occurs is dependent upon the nature of the leaving group and the nucleophile.

     syn– attack   *anti*– attack

Alcohols react with thionyl chloride to furnish chlorides by the intramolecular S_Ni reaction. This process involves front-side nucleophilic attack and means that the carbon undergoing substitution retains its original stereochemistry. Similarly, allylic alcohols undergo S_N1' rearrangement with thionyl chloride to give chlorides by the S_N1' mechanism. Optically active alcohols give optically active chlorides indicating a highly ordered reaction.

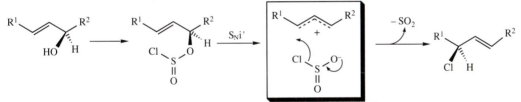

When the incoming nucleophile is the same as the leaving group (for example halide), the end result is a rearrangement of the allylic substrate. In such equilibrations, the ratio of the two products in the final mixture is dependent upon their relative thermodynamic stabilities.

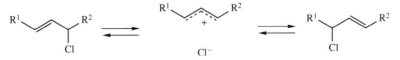

Among the factors which determine the stability of a particular acyclic allylic system are the degree of substitution of the double bond, possibility for conjugation, and steric hindrance. In cyclic allylic systems there are the additional considerations of conformational preference, ring strain, and allylic strain. In an acyclic example, the equilibration between 3-bromoprop-1-ene and 1-bromoprop-2-ene leads to a mixture in which the product with the most substituted double bond predominates.

$$\text{MeCH(Br)CH=CH}_2 \quad \rightleftharpoons \quad \text{MeCH=CHCH}_2\text{Br}$$

The degree of double bond substitution is even more marked when conjugation effects come into play. For instance, the equilibrium between 3-chloro-1-phenylprop-1-ene (cinnamyl chloride) and 3-chloro-3-phenylprop-1-ene (1-phenylallyl chloride) almost completely favours the former.

$$\text{PhCH=CHCH}_2\text{Cl} \quad \rightleftharpoons \quad \text{PhCH(Cl)CH=CH}_2$$
$$\sim 100\%$$

Thermal equilibraton of the phthalate half esters of *syn-* and *anti-* 5-methylcyclohex-2-en-1-ol leads to a mixture in which the *anti-* isomer predominates. This isomer is more stable as it can adopt a conformation in which both ring substituents lie in quasi-equatorial environments.

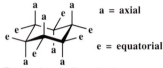

a = axial

e = equatorial

Remember: bulky substituents on a cyclohexane ring prefer to be equatorial. This principal can also be approximately applied to cyclohexene systems, although the ring is more distorted and *allylic strain* may also play an important rôle.

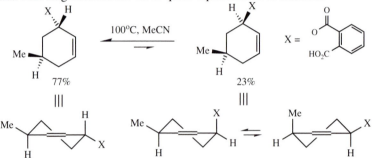

When optically active *syn*-3-chloro-5-methylcyclohexene was solvolysed in ethanol and the rate of solvolysis measured both titrimetrically and polarimetrically, it was found that the polarimetrically determined rate was faster than that obtained by measuring the amount of HCl liberated. This was interpreted as involving initial ionisation to form a tight ion pair which may either lead on to a free carbocation which is attacked by solvent or undergo recombination. Due to the symmetrical nature of the allylic carbocation, there is an equal likelihood of internal return of chloride to either position giving racemic starting chloride.

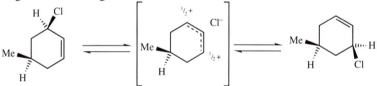

Rearrangements which would migrate a double bond to an exocyclic position appear to be disfavoured. This effect is presumably a consequence of steric compression of the sp^2-carbon angle when it is constrained within a ring compared to an acyclic environment. This is graphically illustrated by the fact that, although tertiary allylic alcohols are generally very rapidly rearranged in acid, this is not the case if such an isomerisation would make the double bond exocyclic.

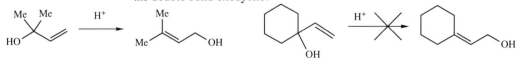

Allylic esters

Depending upon reaction conditions, the rearrangement of allylic esters may occur either by a dissociation–reassociation process to give solvent caged or totally separated ionic species, or by an intramolecular process. As a result of studies on uncatalysed rearrangements of aryl esters of 1- and 3-phenylprop-3-en-1-ol, Burton and Ingold decided that the process involved total heterolytic cleavage followed by recombination.

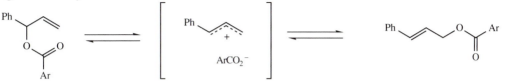

The evidence for this came from their observations that the ease of rearrangement was increased by the presence of electron withdrawing groups on the aryl group and by carrying the reaction out in ionising solvents. They were also able to demonstrate that addition of other nucleophilic species could divert the reaction giving both rearranged and unrearranged substitution products. All of these results provided strong evidence for the existence of free ions. In further support of this conclusion, Meisenheimer demonstrated the reaction to be first order in ester.

However, later studies with specifically labelled substrates showed that the acyl oxygen of the starting ester largely became the alkyl oxygen in the rearranged product. In addition, it was found that, although addition of labelled common anions to the mixture led to some incorporation into both the starting material and rearranged product, the rate of rearrangement was more rapid than incorporation into the rearranged material. This led to the conclusion that rearrangement was occurring largely *via* an internal delivery mechanism in which a large degree of ionic character exists at the transition state.

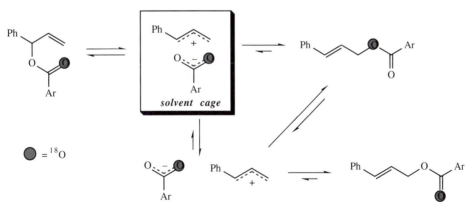

Further support for the existence of an internal delivery system was obtained from the rearrangement of the ^{18}O-carbonyl labelled 4-nitrobenzoate ester of optically active pent-2-en-4-ol which would lead to the enantiomeric material on rearrangement. It was found that the rate of distribution of oxygen label between alkyl and acyl positions was only about a third as fast as racemisation.

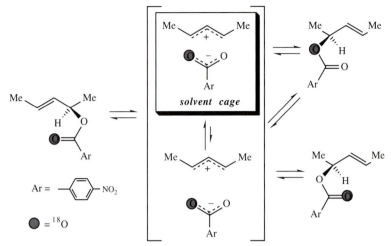

In contrast to uncatalysed rearrangements of allylic esters, acid catalysed processes always appear to occur *via* dissociation and reassociation of the protonated species. For example, rearrangement of optically active 1-phenylprop-2-enyl ^{14}C-acetate in unlabelled acetic acid resulted in isotopic scrambling and racemisation of both product and recovered starting material.

Maeyer–Schuster and related rearrangements

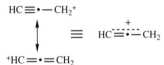

Resonance stabilisation in the allenyl–propynyl cation.

The propynyl (propargyl) cation can also profit from resonance stabilisation in the same way as the allyl cation. However, in this case the alternative extreme resonance canonical form is the allenyl cation and this is not such an important contributor to the resonance hybrid. Nevertheless, propynylic alcohols undergo acid catalysed rearrangements in a manner directly analogous to the corresponding allylic alcohols, with the distinction that the resultant allenic alcohols undergo subsequent tautomerism to form α,β-unsaturated carbonyl compounds in a reaction known as the *Meyer–Schuster rearrangement*.

The mechanism of the rearrangement probably involves a dissociation–reassociation mechanism. Evidence for this comes from the observation of an alternative pathway, the *Rupe rearrangement* in certain substrates. In this variant, deprotonation of the propynylic cation precedes reassociation and this is followed by simple Markownikoff hydration of the alkyne.

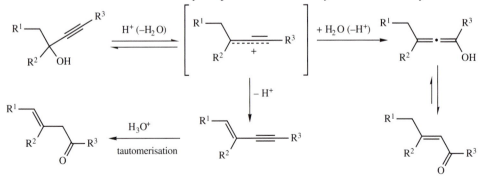

Rupe rearrangement   *Meyer–Schuster rearrangement*

A base catalysed variant of the Meyer–Schuster rearrangement is also known and this has been shown to occur via the expected S_N2' mechanism. Propynylic chlorides may be rearranged to allenic chlorides in the presence of copper (I) chloride, and optically active propynylic alcohols have been shown to react with thionyl chloride to furnish optically active allenes *via* an internal delivery mechanism.

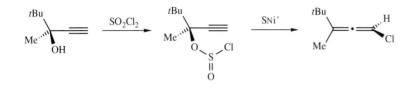

7.3 Polar 2,3-sigmatropic rearrangements

Rearrangement of allylic sulphur and nitrogen ylids

We have already come across examples of 1,2-rearrangements of sulphur and nitrogen ylids in the chapter on electrophilic rearrangements (pp. 61–63). Allylic sulphur and nitrogen ylids can rearrange *via* concerted 2,3-sigmatropic rearrangements to form allylic thioethers and amines respectively.

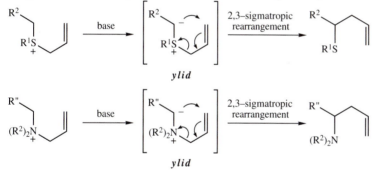

2,3-Wittig rearrangement

The 2,3-sigmatropic rearrangement of the α-anions derived from allylic ethers to furnish homoallylic alcohols is directly analogous with the 1,2-Wittig rearrangement and has already been briefly described on page 64.

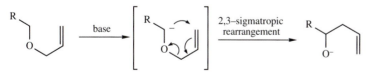

Sulphoxide–sulphenate rearrangement

Heating allylic sulphoxides results in a 2,3-sigmatropic rearrangement to form a sulphenate. For primary and secondary allylic sulphoxides the equilibrium favours the sulphoxide, but rearrangement can be forced to completion if the sulphoxide is heated in the presence of a sulphur trapping agent such as a trialkyl phosphite. Under these conditions rearranged allylic alcohols can be isolated in synthetically useful yields.

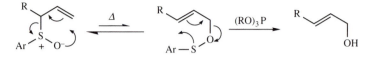

7.4 Polar radical mediated rearrangements

The Hofmann–Löffler–Freytag reaction

Radical rearrangements are typically apolar processes, but the Hofmann–Löffler–Freytag reaction, which involves the radical mediated rearrangement of amine derivatives in the presence of strong acids, must occur *via* the protonated species.

Heating *N*-haloamines possessing a hydrogen at C-4 or C-5 in the presence of acid results in a radical mediated rearrangement to form the 4- or 5-haloamine which can be converted into the corresponding pyrrolidine or piperidine on subsequent mild base treatment. Photochemical and peroxide initiation of the reaction is also possible.

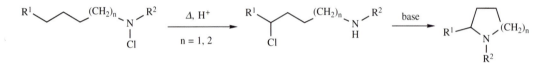

The mechanism involves a radical chain reaction which is initiated by protonation of the nitrogen, and propagated by homolytic cleavage of the *N*-halogen bond followed by hydrogen atom removal from C-4 or C-5.

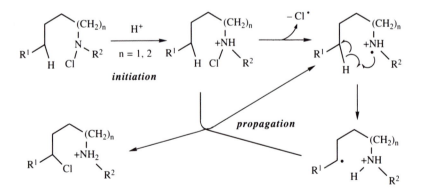

This reaction is very useful as it permits functionalisation of relatively distant, unactivated methylene groups. It is very similar to other radical processes, such as the *Barton reaction* of nitrite esters to give oximes and the rearrangement of *N*-haloamides to form γ-lactones.

7.5 Boron to carbon migrations

Rearrangements of alkyl boranes

Trialkylboranes react with carbon monoxide at elevated temperatures in the presence of ethane-1,2-diol to form a 2-borato-1,3-dioxalane. Oxidative cleavage of the carbon–boron bond results in the formation of a tertiary alcohol. The mechanism has been shown to involve a series of three intramolecular 1,2-nucleophilic alkyl shifts from boron to the carbon *via* intermediate organoborates or *ate complexes*. The migrations occur with retention of the absolute configuration of the alkyl groups.

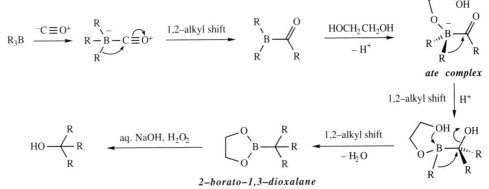

Cyclic boranes derived from hydroboration of dienes or trienes are converted to cyclic alcohols by this route which has been termed *ring stitching* with boron by the Nobel Prize winning chemist H. C. Brown.

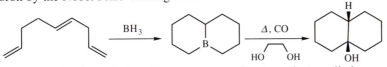

If the reaction is carried out in the presence of water only two alkyl groups migrate to form an intermediate dihydroxy compound which may be decomposed with alkali to form a secondary alcohol. When the borane possesses different alkyl groups, the relative migratory aptitudes are in the order primary > secondary > tertiary. The (1,1,2-trimethyl)propyl substituent (commonly referred to as the '*thexyl*' group) is frequently used for reactions where specific migration of other substituents is required. The only experimental disadvantage in this case is the necessity for using high pressures for the initial carbonylation step.

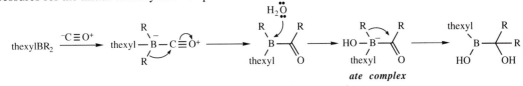

A borohydride reducing agent present in the reaction mixture can intercept the first alkyl migration intermediate to form a primary alcohol.

Rearrangement of vinylboranes

Treatment of vinylboranes with iodine in the presence of base results in the formation of an alkene in which an alkyl group has undergone 1,2-nucleophilic migration from the boron. Migration occurs with retention of absolute stereochemistry of the alkyl group and the alkene is formed with defined geometry. This stereospecificity is a consequence of the mechanism which involves initial formation of an iodonium species, followed by migration and *anti*-elimination of the alkylboron diiodide.

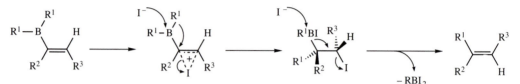

α-Halovinylboranes which may be obtained from the reaction of dialkylboranes with 1-haloalkynes undergo base promoted 1,2-alkyl group migration from the boron to furnish vinylboranes.

These two processes may be carried out in tandem to permit the direct conversion of 1-haloalkynes to trisubstituted alkenes.

Rearrangements of alkynyltrialkylborates

Trialkylboranes react with alkynyl lithium reagents to form borate complexes which undergo 1,2-alkyl migration from boron on treatment with iodine to produce a disubstituted alkyne. The mechanism for this conversion is directly analogous to the vinyl case.

$$(R^1)_3B \xrightarrow{\;R^2 \!=\!\!=\!\! Li\;} R^2 \!=\!\!=\!\! \overset{-}{B}(R^1)_3 \; Li^+ \xrightarrow{\;I_2\;} R^2 \!=\!\!=\!\! R^1$$

Treatment of the borate complex with a carboxylic acid instead of iodine results in the formation of an alkene.

$$R^1 \!=\!\!=\!\! \overset{-}{B}(R^2)_3 \; Li^+ \xrightarrow{\;H^+\;} \cdots \xrightarrow{} \cdots \xrightarrow{\;H^+\;} R^1HC\!=\!CHR^2$$

7.6 The Nazarov cyclisation

This reaction refers to the acid catalysed cyclisation of divinyl ketones.

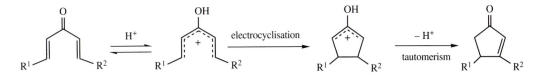

The protonated divinyl ketone undergoes a thermally allowed conrotatory electrocyclisation followed by deprotonation and tautomerisation to form the cyclopentenone product. The final position of the double bond in the cyclic product can be dependent upon the degree of substitution. However, a silicon variant of the Nazarov reaction has been developed in which the ability of silicon to stabilise β-cations controls the position of the double bond.

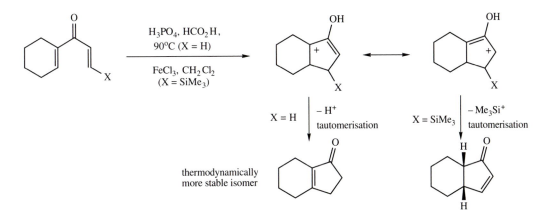

Vinyl allyl ketones may also undergo this rearrangement after initial isomerisation to the divinyl compound.

7.7 The Pummerer rearrangement

Treatment of sulphoxides with acids results in their conversion to hemithioacetal derivatives which can be hydrolysed to carbon compounds. The mechanism involves protonation or acylation of the sulphoxide oxygen, followed by an elimination to form the sulphenium ion which undergoes readdition at the α-position. The Pummerer rearrangement involves a full dissociative process and added nucleophiles may compete successfully with the original leaving group.

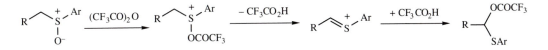

7.8 Exercises

1. Indicate the conversions involved in the following sequences:

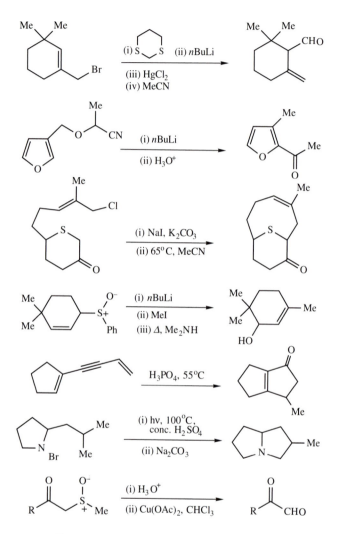

Further reading

For full treatments of allylic rearrangements see: P. D. B. de la Mare, *Molecular Rearrangements*, ed. P. deMayo, Interscience, New York, 1963, Vol. 1, Chapter 2; R. H. DeWolfe, *Comprehensive Chemical Kinetics*, ed. C. H. Bamford and C. F. H. Tipper, Elsevier, New York, 1973, Vol. 9. pp. 417–37.

The Meyer–Schuster and Rupe rearrangements have been reviewed by S. Swamithan and K. V. Narayanan, *Chem. Rev*, 1971, **71**, 160.

For a review of stereochemical aspects of 2,3-sigmatropic rearrangements see: R. W. Hoffmann, *Angew Chem., Int. Ed. Engl.*, 1979, **18**, 563.

The Hoffmann–Löffler–Freytag reaction has been the subject of extensive discussion. For further reading see: L. Stella, *Angew. Chem., Int. Ed. Engl.,* 1983, **22**, 337; M. E. Wolff, *Chem. Rev.*, 1963, **64**, 55.

Boron to carbon migrations are concisely reviewed by S. E. Thomas, *Organic Synthesis, The Roles of Boron and Silicon*, Oxford Chemistry Primers, Oxford University Press 1991, pp. 18–21, and J. March, *Advanced Organic Chemistry, Reactions, Mechanisms and Structure*, 3rd edn., Wiley, New York, 1985, pp. 995–1002. Other works include: A. Suzuki, *Top. Curr. Chem.*, 1983, **112**, 67; A. Pelter, *Chem. Soc. Rev.*, 1982, **11**, 191; G. M. L. Cragg, *Organoboranes in Organic Synthesis*, Marcel Dekker, New York, 1973, pp. 249–300.

The Nazarov cyclisation has been reviewed by C. Santelli–Rouvier and M. Santelli, *Synthesis*, 1983, 429.

The Pummerer rearrangement has been surveyed by S. Oae and T. Numata, *Isot. Org. Chem.*, 1980, **5**, 45 and B. P. Mundy and M. G. Ellerd, *Name Reactions and Reagents in Organic Synthesis*, Wiley, New York, 1988, pp. 174–175.

Index

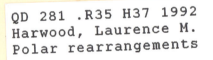